BREAKING THE SILENCE

African POETRY BOOK SERIES

Series editor: Kwame Dawes

BREAKING THE SILENCE

ANTHOLOGY OF LIBERIAN POETRY

Edited by Patricia Jabbeh Wesley

University of Nebraska Press / Lincoln

Acknowledgments for the use of copyrighted
material appear on pages 259–64, which constitute
an extension of the copyright page.

The University of Nebraska Press is part of a land-
grant institution with campuses and programs on the
past, present, and future homelands of the Pawnee,
Ponca, Otoe-Missouria, Omaha, Dakota, Lakota, Kaw,
Cheyenne, and Arapaho Peoples, as well as those of the
relocated Ho-Chunk, Sac and Fox, and Iowa Peoples.

The African Poetry Book Series is operated by the African
Poetry Book Fund. The APBF was established in 2012 with
initial support from philanthropists Laura and Robert
F. X. Sillerman. The founding director of the African
Poetry Book Fund is Kwame Dawes, Holmes University
Professor and Glenna Luschei Editor of *Prairie Schooner*.

Library of Congress Cataloging-in-Publication Data
Names: Wesley, Patricia Jabbeh, editor.
Title: Breaking the silence : anthology of Liberian
poetry / edited by Patricia Jabbeh Wesley.
Description: Lincoln : University of Nebraska Press,
2023. | Series: African poetry book series
Identifiers: LCCN 2022042567
ISBN 9781496233066 (paperback)
ISBN 9781496235916 (epub)
ISBN 9781496235923 (pdf)
Subjects: LCSH: Liberian poetry (English) |
BISAC: POETRY / African | LCGFT: Poetry.
Classification: LCC PR9384.6 .B74 2023 | DDC
821.008/096662—dc23/eng/20220906
LC record available at https://lccn.loc.gov/2022042567

Set and Designed in Garamond Premier Pro
by Mikala R. Kolander.

This book is dedicated to my mother,

Hne Dahtedor Mary Williams, and

all the other mothers of Liberia

CONTENTS

ACKNOWLEDGMENTS

A Penn State University 2020–21 Humanities Institute Residency Award, a one-semester sabbatical, along with various small grants from Penn State Altoona over four years provided support and freed me to begin and complete work on this anthology. Thanks to my division head, Dr. Brian Black, and Penn State Altoona for their support. Thanks to Dr. D. Elwood Dunn, retired professor of politics, author, and Liberian statesman, who gave me several old texts that would form part of this anthology. My gratitude to Friends of Young Scholars of Liberia, a social media group that helped fuel my vision to travel to Liberia over a five-year period in order to mentor, teach, and motivate young Liberians to write their stories. Gratitude to my son, Mlen-Too Wesley II, and other family members who provided me lodging and transportation in Liberia and supported my vision in many ways. I am also indebted to my friends, volunteers, mentees, and young Liberians: Ms. Jee-Won Arkoi, Mr. Augustine Arkoi, and his family; Madam Miatta Fahnbulleh, my confidant and friend, for providing transportation and gas for my long journey to Harper by road that first year; and to my YSL mentees, Aaron Ireland, Vermon Washington, Kulah Washington, and other young Liberians for their tireless skills in organizing my writing workshops for Liberian youth over the years. My appreciation to the readers and text transcribers: Professor Althea Romeo-Mark in Switzerland, Ms. Essah Diaz Cortez, Mo Sheriff, Eva Acqui in Romania, and Enisio Cooper.

Thanks also to the families of deceased Liberian authors, especially Mr. Ruel Dempster, who gave me several texts I needed, Mr. Sando Moore, the family of H. Carey Thomas, Rev. Father James David Kwee Baker, Professor Kona Khasu (James Roberts), and many others who connected me to various families for permission to republish the works of important Liberian writers long dead. As always, I thank my husband, Dr. Mlen-Too Wesley, who hosted me at the William V. S. Tubman University every year between 2016 and 2019 and supported my writing projects with Young Scholars of Liberia in Maryland County, southeastern Liberia. Thanks to faculty and staff at WVST, including Ms. Iona Thomas, whose devotion to this project affirmed my vision for editing this anthology. I am also indebted to Sister Mary Laurene Browne, the then-president of Stella Maris Polytechnic in Monrovia, Liberia, whose moral and in-kind support was invaluable to our writing projects. To my many friends who gave of their financial support to pay for workshop materials and transportation for young Liberian students, I say thanks. This project would not have succeeded without your support. Finally, I am always indebted to our own brother, poet, founder of African Poetry Book Series, Professor Kwame Dawes, who always listens, cautions, advises, and sacrifices for African and African diaspora literature and writers. Thanks for your guidance.

INTRODUCTION

African literary scholars, researchers, and students of African literature have wondered for many decades where Liberia is in the African literary canon, some posing this very question to me at annual conventions when I meet them. I too have pondered this question since grade school. I read numerous African novels, poetry books, even literary critics like Eldred Jones, anything I could get my hands on, but found nothing in my country that rose to the level of these critics. Every anthology on African poetry I read left me shocked at the lack of any representation from us. On the other hand, in college, I studied the works of Liberian authors, but on critical examination, I discovered that these were mostly self-published, non-peer-reviewed pamphlets or small books, read only in Liberia. The silence was deafening. Liberian writers are so invisible, even after publishing six books of my own poetry over twenty-two years, editors of African anthologies are still conditioned to leaving me out. Our silence seems to have erased Liberia off the literary map.

Liberia is a small country that was founded when repatriated freed slaves from the American South landed on the west coast of Africa, fought many battles with Indigenous African peoples who inhabited the region, and declared the country independent in 1847. With the exception of Ethiopia, Liberia became the oldest republic on the African continent. With more than 175 years of independence to date, however, Liberia has had very little body of literature or artistic tradition to show for this great age. In other words, Liberia did not produce an internationally recognized body of literature or literary giants until the 1990s. This puzzling reality evoked in me the dream of becoming that literary giant that we lacked. I dreamed of writing life into Liberia; whether or not that dream has come true is your judgement.

Do not misunderstand me; I grew up in a country with tremendous talent. From an examination of Liberia's oral literature (a West African tradition that is becoming lost in this age) and the works of early writers, there is no doubt that Liberians have always been talented in poetry and orality. Had the framers of Liberia given serious attention to their own abilities, we could have seen more out of Liberia. While we value the efforts of nationally known writers publishing non-peer-reviewed books prior to the 1990s, it is clear that we failed to produce literature worthy of recognition on the world stage for more than a century and a half. The lack of national publishing houses or presses and any governmental support further exacerbated the problem for Liberian writers and poets. We did not and could not produce our own versions of the literary giants publishing across Africa in the postcolonial years.

African writers whose nations gained independence from European colonizers in the late 1950s and 1960s, more than a century after Liberia declared itself independent, were producing internationally renowned literature by the mid-1960s. Where were our Chinua Achebe, Wole Soyinka, Camara Laye, our Flora Nwapa, Buchi Emecheta? Was this lack of a serious literary tradition or a push to develop our literature a symptom of our conflicting history as the only country in Africa settled by the American Colonization Society? Was this identity crisis (where to be Native or African was frowned on) the source of our lack of growth in the defining elements of a nation—art and literature?

Liberia's conflicting history produced many complex realities that limited what we became as a nation; what artistic forms we represent, Native or settler culture; our visual art forms; our music, traditional or Western; and our literature or how our literary voices articulate our reality as Africans or settlers. This conflict between the Indigenous majority's self-identity and the identity imposed on them by the new founders and leaders limited how Liberians thought of themselves in Africa. The 1960s ushered Liberia out of the so-called dark Africa into a new day of the West African region, which was emerging as a powerful pan-African reality in the Back-to-Africa revolution after independence from European colonizers. In this new reality where Liberia continued to pride itself as Africa's oldest independent nation even while holding on tightly to its roots in slavery, Ghana, Nigeria, and other countries around the continent were turning away from westernization and the stronghold of colonialism. Liberian leadership's skewed vision for themselves as freed slaves landing on a continent from which their ancestors were forcefully captured and taken away, this American South mindset of the master-slave vision for Africa, however, left Liberia with a crippling identity crisis that would influence how our literature or history was written or not written into the twenty-first century.

After nearly two centuries of existence, Liberia is still a country with many conflicting realities, not only about our literature but also our culture and our identity as a people having inherited a dual culture of the newcomer settlers from the American South (who called themselves Americo-Liberian or Conger people) and of the Indigenous African majority. Ironically, the majority culture was mostly rejected and marginalized by the ruling Americo-Liberian elites. Was this conflicting identity crisis responsible for the lack of our own literary heroes or the development of our own art forms, our own songs that should have been rooted in an African identity, and the marginalization of our cultural traditions? This first comprehensive anthology, *Breaking the Silence: Anthology of Liberian Poetry*, will take you through a partial view of the Liberian literary journey and also give you a small view into Liberia's history, something all good literature does.

Before this anthology, there was an earlier attempt at editing a comprehensive volume of Liberian poetry by an American expatriate, A. Doris Banks Henries. Henries not only married, inarguably, the most powerful political figure in Liberia but also carved out a distorted history of Liberia through her numerous books and pamphlets. Her books provided the roadmap of the elite Liberian leadership's vision of Indigenous peoples. Two of her books, *Civics for Liberian Schools* (1966) and *The Liberian Nation:*

A Short History (1954), helped indoctrinate the country's youth about the "savages," "native tribes," "primitive" people, and pioneers seeking liberty. In her introduction to the only other anthology of Liberian poetry, *Poems of Liberia, 1836–1961* (1963), she wrote, "Returning to the land of their ancestors, the pioneer settlers from America found themselves in the midst of savage tribes." Henries, a U.S. citizen, became the most powerful writer in poetry and prose, telling our stories the way the slave master tells the story of his slaves. Her biased account of our history drowned many other literary voices up to the 1980 Liberian military coup, when she fled the country.

Art in all of its forms, including music, dance, theater, and literature, is important to the survival of every culture and people. And that art must be authentic and relevant to the people. Despite the myths propagated by early Western colonizers that Africa was a place devoid of culture or art forms, we, indeed, have had a culture rich in art for centuries. Our cultural foundation as a people on the continent is intertwined with art. And art in Africa is not art for art's sake as in the Western world. Literature in Africa must be a social, cultural, and, most often, political force, meant to enhance the society's well-being. Our music, village songs, and plays; our drumming, masks, and other art forms; our folklore, dirges, myths, and legends; our enduring oral traditions and storytelling heritage that are centuries old are the pillars that today's writers, musicians, visual artists, and literary artists have relied on as their source of creativity. However, when a new nation is founded by people who see themselves as Americans coming to "civilize the savages" (even though they supposedly came for freedom from slavery), such conflicting cultural perspectives can hinder that nation's development of the very art forms I have described above.

Up until a century and half after independence, however, everything African and Indigenous was frowned upon, even our dirges and songs, our poetic forms, Indigenous languages, our African names, our dress forms—our very identity as Africans was rejected, pushed aside by the leaders of this new nation founded by freed slaves as they promoted everything Western and American. Was this a political strategy since African literature does not divorce itself from the sociopolitical reality of the people, or was this just an oversight by our founders?

I am exploring these issues because one cannot understand the silence in Liberia's literary representation on the continent without understanding the identity crisis I have outlined. One cannot understand why we need to "Break the Silence" without exploring these ironies. As I said earlier, the region known today as Liberia was home to African oral traditions that have fed African literature for centuries. Long before the arrival of the settlers, this region was populated by our Indigenous peoples, rich in the oral, cultural traditions that protected and preserved our art forms. The oral storytelling culture of the Grebo, Kru, Kpelle, Mano, Gio, Gola, Vai, Dey, Bassa, Lorma, Mandingo, Kissi, Belle, and Kissi people contributed to the new nation at its founding. Liberian literature did not begin in 1847. Reading Henries's anthology, however, you would think that we had no poetry prior to the arrival of the settlers. Was this lack due to the rejection of our African culture in the framing of Liberia?

On the other hand, an examination of Liberia's earliest written poetry by the Americo-Liberian ordained leadership of the new republic reveals the conflicting history of our literary tradition. Someone told me once that the early poets prior to and after 1847 wrote only in Western forms because "this was what they knew." But I would rather say that they wrote in Western form despite what they could have learned from the new homeland they were carving out and from African peoples they met on these shores of Africa.

After over 175 years, here is a more comprehensive anthology of Liberian poetry. My idea of collecting and editing a book of Liberian poetry was birthed after twenty years of publishing my own collections of poetry in the United States and living with the reality that my home country was still basically invisible on the African literary landscape. My books have ushered me into the international spotlight, have placed Liberia on the literary map of Africa and the world, but like our proverb says, "One tree does not make a forest." I needed to collect and edit the works of Liberian poets who mostly were not published in any anthologies or collections. We needed an anthology that would bring together all of us, poets from our very beginning to the present. That dream drove me to work with young, talented, aspiring Liberian poets struggling to make sense of their world. For five years, I visited Liberia during the summers and during my sabbatical to teach young writers how to better tell their own stories in poetry. To put together a comprehensive body of poetry, I needed their voices too. I also needed to teach them how to write like Liberians and like Africans. *Breaking the Silence: Anthology of Liberian Poetry* is therefore a comprehensively diverse book that tells our story through the voices of the early settlers, the revolutionary 1960s, the turbulent 1980s of military coups, and the brutal war years of the 1990s to the 2020s. Ours is not a massive volume of works but a story that has never been told before. To break the silence, we have to do it with our diversity—the Indigenous, the founding settlers, who sing of finding freedom from the bondage of slavery, and also my forefathers, who are the indigenous. Such a book must also include we who are descendants of African tribes, rejected and marginalized, children of the newcomers, as well as aspiring poets, the inheritors of our complex, conflicting realities that drove us into bloody warfare, for which some of us are now called diaspora Liberians.

The book is divided into four sections: Part 1, "Early Liberian Poetry, 1800–1959," spans from the politician Hilary Teage, who like his contemporaries wrote about his journey from America without focusing on poetry as a career, to the very talented poet and politician Edwin James Barclay, Liberia's eighteenth president. The overpowering poetic voice of the period, Barclay saw the need to put together his work in a pamphlet edition, capturing his diversity of talent, writing about the nation they were struggling to build and the women who broke his heart. The poets of part 1 wrote in Western form about their place as the nation's leaders. Part 2 comprises poets writing during the 1960s, a period that saw its first Indigenous poets and a change in Liberian poetics. "Liberian Poetry, 1960–1989" extends from the end of the William V. S. Tubman years of political praise poems to their presidents into the 1980 military coup. This period saw a breakthrough of poets focusing on the Liberian landscape, our oceans, our being as Liberians, and the Liberian pepper bird, an enduring motif. These poets were more committed to writing, although they had to work fulltime to make a living, like their predecessors. Part 2 consists of poets writing from the 1960s to the 1980s, the more nationally known. Their poetics nourished my generation that learned to write in the turbulent 1980s.

Roland Tombekai Dempster, Bai T. Moore, and H. Carey Thomas were the major voices in this period. Even though the poetry of H. Carey Thomas was not so well known in Liberia, he was a political figure who headed the ruling party for decades, a poet whose voice would have been well received even outside of Africa had he had a collection published. Bai T. Moore, also a political leader and an advocate of Liberian culture, was the most well-known poet in the country, publishing his collection *Ebony Dust* in 1962. These three figures in the period broke away from their predecessors by exploring the country that had not been a focus for poetry. Most of their predecessors, including Barclay and Warner, had been preoccupied with their heritage as American settlers charged to lead a nation and becoming president, instead of being just poets.

Part 3, "Contemporary Liberian Poetry, 1990–Present," comprises writers who were experimenting with poetry in the turbulent, militarized 1980s and became more widely published from the 1990 war years into the twenty-first century, producing writers like K. Moses Nagbe, Althea Romeo-Mark, and myself, Patricia Jabbeh Wesley, the author of now six collections of poetry. Althea-Romeo Mark, an American Caribbean expatriate in Liberia, would become part of this Liberian literary movement that worked to reframe what Liberian poetry was to be, experimenting in the late 1980s to 1990s and into the war years. This generation could boast of many writers, but several did not make it into the anthology.

Part 4, "Emerging and Aspiring Liberian Poets," includes a new generation of Liberian poets, young, vibrant, and engaged in telling their own stories about inheriting a war they never saw and living in the ruins and poverty of postwar, stagnant Liberia. They are eager to develop their craft in the now more global world of Africans without a country, the new world of the global writer. I dream they will pick up from me and from us, from their founding fathers, who sang of having come "to these shores of Africa to civilize the savages" and left them bereft of any literary footprints. These young people, fortunate to be included in a major anthology, are helping to break the silence by the talking drums of poetry, our enduring African talking drum that has too long been mute.

BREAKING THE SILENCE

PART I

Early Liberian Poetry, 1800–1959

Land of the Mighty Dead

HILARY TEAGE

Land of the mighty dead,
here, Science once displayed,
dart, her charms.
Here, awful Pharaohs swayed
great nations who obeyed.

Here, distant monarchs laid
their vanquished arms.

They hold us in survey.
They cheer us on our way.
They loud proclaim
from Pyramidal hall,
from Carnac's sculptured wall,
from Thebes they loudly call,
retake your fame!

All hail Liberia, hail!
Arise and now prevail
o'er all thy foes.
In truth and righteousness,
in all the arts of peace
advance, and still increase
though hosts oppose.

At the loud call, we rise
and press towards the prize
in glory's race:

All redolent of fame,
the land to which we came.
We'll breathe the inspiring flame
and onward press.

Here liberty shall dwell.
Here justice shall prevail.
Religion here.
To this fair virtue's dome,
meek innocence may come,
and find a peaceful home
and know no fear.
Oppression's cursed yoke,
by freeman shall be broke,
in dust be laid,
the soul erect and free.
Here evermore shall be
to none we'll bend the knee,
but nature's God.

Proud science here shall rear
her monuments, to bear
with deathless tongue.
By nations yet unborn
her glories shall be known,
and art her tribute join,
the praise prolong.

Commerce shall lift her head
to suspicious gales shall spread
expanded wing.
From India's spicy land,

from Europe's rock-bound strand,
from Peru's golden sand
her tribute brings.

Oh Lord we look to Thee.
To Thee, for help, we flee.
Lord, hear our prayer:
in righteousness, arise,
scatter our enemies,
their hellish plots surprise
and drive them far.

Oh, happy people they
who Israel's God obey,
where Lord is God:
They shall be blest indeed,
from anxious cares be freed.
And for them is decreed
a large reward.

Liberia Herald, DECEMBER 23, 1843

Hymn

HILARY TEAGE

We sing the wondrous deeds of Him,
who rides upon the sky.
His name is God, the glorious theme
is sung by saints on high.

His days are one eternal now.
His kingdom has no bound.
Before his feet archangels bow
in reverence profound.
He guides revolving years; He sits
high on the circling skies.
In glory, majesty and might,
o'erpowering angels' eyes.

We were by those beset around,
who craved to drink our blood,
whose malice, hatred knew no bound,
whose hearts of love were void.

Hark from afar the trumpets send
the dreadful notes of war,
and tinkling bells, and drums, portend
a bloody conflict near.

The savage yell, the dreadful cry,
fell on our frighted ear.
The gleaming spear, the clam'ring throng,
with terror did appear.

Their Gods of wood and stone they trust,
to give success in fight.
The warrior and the stupid priest
to murder here unite.

To God we cried, Lord hear our prayer
in this our deep distress,
we have none but Thee: His ear
Attended to our case.

He spoke, the savage has retired.
He looked, and deep dismay
seized those who were with courage fired.
Like smoke, they fled away.

"Be still," He said, "for I am He,
that's powerful to save,
for all that put their trust in me
shall full deliverance have."

Why do the foolish heathen rage?
Why do they thus unite?
Why in these hellish leagues engage
against our land to fight?

Nor might, nor wisdom of an arm,
to speak we now unite.
All praise we give to Him alone
who taught our hands to fight.

DECEMBER 1, 1836

"All Hail, Liberia Hail," Liberian National Anthem

DANIEL BASHIEL WARNER

All hail, Liberia, hail! (All hail!)
All hail, Liberia, hail! (All hail!)
This glorious land of liberty,
shall long be ours.
Though new her name,
green be her fame,
and mighty be her powers.
And mighty be her powers.
In joy and gladness,
with our hearts united,
we'll shout the freedom,
of a race benighted.
Long live Liberia, happy land!
A home of glorious liberty,
by God's command!
A home of glorious liberty,
by God's command!

All hail, Liberia, hail! (All hail!)
All hail, Liberia, hail! (All hail!)
In union strong success is sure,
we cannot fail!
With God above,
our rights to prove,
we will o'er all prevail,
we will o'er all prevail!
With heart and hand our country's cause defending,
we'll meet the foe with valor unpretending.

Long live Liberia, happy land!
A home of glorious liberty,
by God's command!
A home of glorious liberty,
by God's command!

Wishing to Be "21"

DANIEL BASHIEL WARNER

On life's gay morn when all is peace,
and wasting cares have not our ease
nor sun of patience tried,
in thought we haste, we run to gain
the painted mount beyond the plain
of manhood's pride.

Nor friends nor fathers we heed,
but to our fancy still add speed,
impatient to be gone,
beyond the bounds of love's restraints
and all she's pledged to make as saints,
and save us hopes forlorn.

Towards that mount of twenty-one,
with wild activity we run
and solace all our own,
enraptured near to ecstasy,
we bound away, in haste to see,
ourselves to manhood grown.

With stubborn will, our course we go,
we spurn the humble plain below,
however sweet its flowers,
up that bright painted mount we climb,
fancy its summit all sublime,
its woods the best of bowers.

'Tis thus we dream with open eyes,
begging each moment as it flies.
To bear up to that borne
of manhood's stern reality,
which ends in bold Eternity,
whence we shall ne'er return.

But when that tempting mount is won,
and all its charms that lured us on
are seen with their sad train,
backward in in bitter thought we turn
to scenes our folly bade us spurn,
and wish us boys again.

Too late, the sun of years is told
that makes us one and twenty old,
there's no returning back.
Onward, we grant you no delay,
whatever you may lack.

And now our morn of life is past,
our riper years come on in haste,
all burdened with some care,
buried in grief we sadly scan,
the road that led us up to man,
its joys no more to share.

Heavenly Rest Implored

ROBERT H. GIBSON

O Jesus, I long for my rest,
say, why dost Thou tarry so long?
Thy servant would lean on Thy breast,
and pour out my heart through my song.
When troubles assail me—I hide,
while billows roll over my head.
My faith in the blood from His side,
brings pleasure and life to my bed.

I would not live always on earth,
away from the God of my love.
Rich pleasures come through the new birth,
a foretaste of Heaven above.
The Spirit and Bride bid me come,
I can't rest contented away.
For Jesus, the Father's dear Son,
calls sinners, and I must obey.

Rise, Take Up Thy Bed and Walk

ROBERT H. GIBSON

Lord, I'm feeble, sick, and sore.
Many years I've been distress'd,
lying here, could do no more
while fierce disease oppress'd.
Thou dost bid me rise, and walk.
Virtue from Thee must flow out
of Thy goodness, I will talk.
Grant faith, I'll cease to doubt.

Many years I've lain in sin,
sickness, sorrow, fierce disease.
Wretched, waiting to get in,
till Christ, my sorrow sees.
Old Bethesda, still in view.
On my couch, I lie in pain
till the Shepherd of the Jew
behold my mangled frame.

Thou hast bidden me arise,
go, "Take up thy bed and walk."
Glad my spirit to Thee flies,
I, of Thy goodness talk.
Long I've lain so near this pool,
seeking for its healing balm.
Hoping, trusting to be whole,
and singing David's Psalm.

Eight and thirty years in grief,
I have linger'd in despair.
Till my Jesus gave relief,
and made me heaven's heir.
Many near the pool stepp'd in,
while stagger'd, weak in pain,
loaded with disease and sin,
I'd start—return the same.

Angels, as the seasons came,
gave the pool its cleansing pow'r.
Th' impotent, and blind, and halt
stepp'd in the needy hour.
Oft I stronger, got before,
my poor soul left in despair,
while they, their God adore.

Jesus met me near the porch,
quite diseased, and in despair,
saw my weakness—my reproach,
and made me heaven's heir.
Sickness of old standing left,
Soul reviv'd and fill'd with light.
Rock of ages for me cleft,
I enter'd, clean and bright.

Hallelujah, —Jesus reigns,
through all ages, just the same.
Gathers millions in His realm,
and bids them there remain.
All I need to make me whole
is His cleansing blood from sin.
Hidden love, that can't be told,
but purifies within.

Song of the First Emigrants to Cape Palmas

ROBERT H. GIBSON

For Africa! For Africa! Our way lies o'er the deep
where ride we crest of briny waves and down their valleys sweep.
We leave behind the white seagulls at limit of their flight,
until around CAPE PALMAS, again we'll greet their sight,
as though the feathered things had flown to welcome us; when we
shall tread, as tread Afric's shore, the footsteps of the free.

For Africa! For Africa! Our flag is floating fair.
We have taken Freedom's banner, though its stars are wanting there.
But, in their place, the holy sign is on the azure field,
and cross and stripes have now become our standard and our shield.
And yet, where Afric's palm trees wave, where whirls the dread simoon,
may mark where pilgrims wending home, may loose their sandal shoon.

For Africa! For Africa! We bear the glorious light
whose radiance from revealed truth is more than sun-beam bright.
Where hearts of wandering thousands no softening thoughts have known,
where prayer has never yet gone up to Heaven's eternal throne,
we'll plant the cross, the idol break, we "teach the sacred word"
until through heathen Africa, our God shall be adored.

For Africa! For Africa! Oh! Who would stay behind?
The anchor hangs upon the bow, the sails swell in the wind.
Our fatherland, the love of thee within our hearts now reigns.
Then bid thy wanderers welcome through all thy boundless plains.
Yield from thy fruitful bosom, a harvest to our toil,
until we find, 'neath shadowing palms, our graves within thy soil.

St Paul's River Liberia

ANONYMOUS

On, on, ye dark waters rolling,
hosting to the blue ocean's waves.
Say say—tell what thou art bearing
far down in the wild ocean's cave.

Down, down thou art constantly pouring
thy fearful, deep, bold turbid tide,
say, say for once what thou art bringing
far away from the Moon's mountain tide.

Stay, stay a moment of staying,
wilt thou, ere thou leavest the main?
Say, say what art thou are bringing
where treasure for ages have lain.

Then, then tell me what thou hast torn
from those rugged mountains of gold,
hidden treasures, fit to be worn,
to the deck the bride of the bold?

Speak, speak to hearts that are humming
while now on thy bosom they ride.
Say, say to loved hearts that are tuning
that no evil to them shall betide.

Aye, aye I hear thee not speaking,
yet a constant slave thou shalt be.
Not gold from mountain, bringing
only, but strong iron from sea.

Soon, soon on thy wave will be coming,
the restless wild-Fire-king of speed.
He, he that by constant is rolling
the fierce stormy ocean and main.

Oh, oh then I'll set to laughing
when he comes purling along
at his storm whistle of warning
and his engine thunder of song.

On, on ye dark waters rolling
soon no rocky falls will remain.
Far the new fire god is upturning
the river, the mountain and plain.

WRITTEN IN MONROVIA, JUNE 30, 1855, FOR THE
Liberia Herald (AUGUST 2, 1855)

The Emigrant's Hymn

PIERRE

I come from the west, from
    the land of the slave.
To freedom's blest land,
    to the land of the brave.
Where base tyranny's yoke
    hath never been wore.
Nor the color'd man's race
    pointed at with scorn.

I am free! I'm as free as
    the air I breathe.
I've none to obey and
    can do as I please.
Liberia's laws I will love
    and respect.
And be to her a good
    and faithful subject.

All hail! Young republic,
    thy years they are few.
But God will protect thee,
    and prosper thee too.
Liberia's flag, long may
    its lone star wave.
O'er this land of the free.
    this home of the brave.

Liberia Herald, JANUARY 7, 1857

The Lone Star

A National Song

EDWIN JAMES BARCLAY

When Freedom raised her glowing form
on Montserrado's verdant height,
she set within the dome of night,
—midst lowering skies and thunderstorm,—
The star of Liberty!
And seizing from the waking morn,
its burnished shield of golden flame,
she lifted it in her proud name,
and roused a nation long forlorn,
to nobler destiny!

REFRAIN

> The lone star forever,
> The lone star forever!
O long may it float o'er land and o'er seas—!
> Desert it! No! Never!
> Uphold it, ay, ever!
O shout for the lone-starred banner, Hurrah!

II

Then speeding in her course, along
    the broad Atlantic's golden strand,
    she woke reverb'rant through the land
A nation's loud triumphant song,—
            the song of Liberty!
And o'er Liberia's altar fires,
    she wide the lone-starred flag unfurled,—
    Proclaimed to an expectant world,

the birth, for Afric's sons and sires,—
The birth of Liberty!—REF.
The lone star forever,
The lone star forever!
O long may it float o'er land and o'er seas—!
Desert it! No! Never!
Uphold it, ay, ever!
O shout for the lone-starred banner, Hurrah!

III

Then, forward, sons of Freedom, March!
Defend the sacred heritage!
The nation's call from age to age
Where'er it sounds 'neath heaven's arch,—
wherever foes assail.
Be ever ready to obey
'Gainst treason and rebellion's front,
'Gainst foul aggression. In the burnt
of battle lay the hero's way!—
All hail, Lone Star, all hail!—REF.
The lone star forever,
The lone star forever!
O long may it float o'er land and o'er seas—!
Desert it! No! Never!
Uphold it, ay, ever!
O shout for the lone-starred banner, Hurrah!

To Pauline—a Flirt

EDWIN JAMES BARCLAY

Fickle and false, most uncertain, and vain
in all thy unwomanly vices and sins.
Luring a man but to doom him to pain,
Flirt, how I scorn now thy blandishments foul!

Deeply I loved thee! Unworthy thou art
to bear the proud title of woman or wife!
Nature's abortion, thou thing without heart!
Thou serpent-tongued monster! Thou slayer of souls!

See how she glories in "tricks of the trade."
See how she angles for the homage of men!
See, when she walks the immodest parade.
She makes of her carriage, her figure, her form!

Down with the monster,—the thing without soul,
that stains the escutcheon of pure womanhood!
Out on it! down with it! Crush it, and roll.
Remnant and atom to winds of the earth!

Thus, do I shew thee thyself as thou art,
Pauline, thou thing that I erstwhile adored,—
A thing without conscience, a soul or a heart,
profuse in caresses, a wanton in love!

To Lygia

EDWIN JAMES BARCLAY

On the tense chords of Life when the warm breath of love
wakes a soft resonance to the heart's deepest prayer,
and the quickening shafts of the Sun-God above
melt the shadows that loom in this life's atmosphere.
Say, O radiant queen of my soul's sacred shrine,
wakes the sister-impulse in that fond heart of thine.

Ofttimes have I stood on some cliff grim and grey,
awaiting in vain spicy zephyrs that bear
the sweet hope of a far more enjoyable day.
And as oft have been duped into thinking I hear
in the sea's deep-toned roar whispered words that will give
permission to hope, and desire to live.

I have chased the wild bees whose sweet droning entice
through long lanes that were decked with chrysanthemum bloom.
I have wandered and prayed and in tears, paid the price
of a vain sentiment, and, alas, 'tis my doom
that my passionate longings,—my soul's deep desire
should all die like the flames of a fuel-less fire.

Pity, pity, O Love, a sad soul's dark distress.
Shed thy smile o'er my life and enliven its stream:
For I lack now for naught save thy blissful caress:
For endearments that make life a long summer's dream,
grant me this, grant me this, O my life, grant me this,
give thy love and seal the rich gift with a kiss!

To Jealous Lygia

EDWIN JAMES BARCLAY

Tell me no more in the deep cup of love
  Never mingle sweet nectar and poison:
Deeply we drink, and strongly we prove
  how its taste brings a strange revelation.
Oft have I sipped from thy cup the sweet draught,
  and as oft have I felt intermingled.
Passions that wept, and soft passions that laughed
  as its streams through my frame swiftly tingled.

Love giveth life, ay, and love giveth death.
  There is none that can fathom the reason.
The blue dome above and the green earth beneath
  sing the very same song every season.
Love is the link that entwineth twin souls;
  It is likewise the gulf that divideth.
Bridge the abyss where Hate's dark river rolls,
  but the poisonous drug still abideth.

Tell me no more that thy love has no dross,
  for I knew, dear sweetheart, thou art jealous.
Knowledge of gain and the dull fear of loss
  to the maelstrom of doubt e'er compel us.
Weary no more with a needless debate.
  It can only portend to thee evil.
Thy lover is true to his former estate,
  and this doubt's but a child of the devil!

Human Greatness

EDWIN JAMES BARCLAY

The starry hosts whose far-flung cohort's gleam
with silvery radiance on the Capes of Night
have quenched their bivouac-fires and in wild flight
are hastening like a panic haunted stream
of crushed battalions. Mighty did they seem—
The flaming bulwarks of eternity—
but now, for their glorious pageantry,
the filmy remnant of a faded dream.
O History, upon thy glowing page
time writes her judgments, but she writes in vain.
Her symbols man misreads in every age,
and garners thence but legacies of pain.
Then why lift up, O man, your heart in pride?
You are but dust, and even Caesar died.

Afric's Lament

EDWIN JAMES BARCLAY

Break! Break! Break! on my rugged shore, O sea!
Dash in furious madness to windward and to lee!
But ne'er canst thou daunt the spirit Ethiopia breathes
      within,
whilst thou bring from proud Europa her vileness and
      her sin!

Waft! Waft! Waft! ye winds from a northern clime,
and bear on your far-brooding pinions the lies of far-
      speeding time.
But how can you hope to enfreshen this soul with your
      stinging blast?
And how can ye hope to enliven, ye murderers in the past?

As long as yon star beams in glory, as long as the sun
      never sets,
as long as there's life for the living and death for him
      who forgets,
do long shall I stand before you, bare-bosomed and most
      defiled,—
A phantom that e'er shall haunt you, O Europe's fairest
      child!

What more can I, giving, grant you? and what have I
      e'er withheld?
Or in these days of darkness or the palmy days of eld?
The offspring of this bosom thou knowest how were torn,
how from my dark brow were stolen the gems that thou
      hast worn!

Thy boasted wealth and power, thy foul ill-gotten gains,
the heritage of bloodshed, of wickedness and chains.
How come they? Ah thou knowest, thou knowest all thy
        sin!
How life is naught but horror where're thine armies win!

Tho' torn and sore and bleeding, I still remain thy prey.
Think not there breaks no morrow,—no fairer, calmer day:
Think not the sleepless heavens no retribution gives,
nor that the God who sleeps not, cares not for those who
        grieve!

Sing well the white man's burden, ay, sing his pleasures
        too!
The pleasures are his portion, the burdens—others rue!
Yea, others pour their lifeblood to quench his sordid greed,
while he lives on unconscious,—unmindful of their need.

Break! Break! Break on my heart, O sea, thy wave!
Bear hitherward Europa, for here she finds her grave!

The Race-Soul

EDWIN JAMES BARCLAY

Say, what, O what of the great race-soul,
  —the soul of the Black and free—
the soul that throbs midst the deepest gloom
  with a true immortality?

Yes, the world rolls on, and the ages pass,
  and life with its thunderous tread,
keeps pace with the rhythm of the soul's deep song
  as we steadily forge ahead!

While it throbs and throbs and the dominant hand
  strikes the chords of affections pure,
there's never the ghost of a base desire,
  or materialistic woe!

Move along, O world, on your sordid plate,
  grasp the wraith of your noon-night dream!
The Black man treads in a surer field
  where no traitorous beauties gleam.

And he measures arms,—but not with men
  of a "base and a low design,"
whoever rejoice in the clink of gold
  and the sparkle of ruddy wine.

Yes, he measures arms, ay, but not with those
    who murder the weak and small;
but he mounts the height of a pure delight
    when he pities the woes of all!

O the fulsome ring of the battle shout,
    wakes no echoes in his breast;
for the Black man hates the turbulent field,—
    the broad field of a great unrest.

The Ocean's Roar

EDWIN JAMES BARCLAY

What spirit lurks in the Ocean's roar
   as it beats the bare breast
   of th' unyielding shore?
'Tis the fierce sprite of a grave unrest,—
Of the madness and th' unending strife
and clash of what man calleth LIFE!

For this did the Father who fashioned all
   that moves on this terrestrial ball—
Give the loud-voiced thunder to the rolling main
That man, hearing oft its reverberant strain,
might sense the true tone of discord and strife—
The epitome of his inharmonious life—
And thus, does the sound of the sea's deep roar
teach us a lesson evermore, evermore!

Dawn

EDWIN JAMES BARCLAY

Far in the East the Sun, whose lambent flames
peep through the purple gauze which hides away
things unforeseen from those already past,
appears his brow: The while, fair imps of light
roll up the filmy sheet 'twixt Night and Day,
and drowsy Nature dons her dew-decked crown,
awakening all to life and work and Love!

Song of the Harmattan

EDWIN JAMES BARCLAY

We are coming, we are coming
    from the vast Sahara plain,
with the iciness of winter,
    and the biting kiss of pain!

We are coming, we are coming!
    Hark! the shrieking echoes rise
over hills, from hidden caverns,
    as we race 'neath tropic skies!

We are coming, we are coming
    with our scourging blasts of pain:
But the fields o'er which we revel
    soon shall blossom fair again!

We are coming!—not a terror!
    Tho men reck not our desire,
tho they shun our wild caresses,
    tho they curse the wild "high-flyer"

We are coming but in earnest
    of the purer atmosphere.
Man shall breathe when foul Miasma
    shall have yielded us his sphere!

We are coming! Greet us kindly.
    We seek out the haunts of pain,
and we carry death for weakness,
    from the vast Sahara plain!

But the strong man is made stronger
    by our penetrating blast.
And the earth is purer, healthier
    when Harmattan's host is past!

The Past

EDWIN JAMES BARCLAY

The Past! the Past! O Love, recall
    its joys, its hopes, its cheerful years;
    its tranquil hours, its short-lived fears,
O Love, recall, recall them all!

The Past! the Past! ah, hadst thou known
    the unsoothed pain, the smarting wound
    which this sad heart in sorrow bound
has felt, would'st thou its joys have flown?

Ah, tell me not the Past is past:
    Such accents cannot quench desire.
    For Hope still lives and riseth higher
where Memory's leaves fall thick and fast.

Ah, tell me not all hope is dead:
    That passing years have crowned our brows
    with fell despair. Recall the vows
of love we made; let hope be fed.

Can love be dead? May passing years,
    pulsed with the throbbing of our hearts,
    drown all the hopes which faith imparts?
Must holy love be quenched in tears?

Ask thine own heart for mine beats fast
    with faith, tho' still unrealized:
    The joyous hopes once dearly prized
live but to crown our life at last!

Let faith, let death, let life and time—
    the minions of eternity,
    the God of Love and destiny,
teach thee, my heart, this faith sublime.

PART II

Liberian Poetry, 1960–1989

O Maryland! Dear Maryland!

REV. FATHER JAMES DAVID KWEE BAKER

What beauty greets the eyes that see
    thy rocky cape extend to sea!
Thy billowy waves that bleach the stones,
    resounding thou their welcome tones.
    O Maryland! Dear Maryland!
    a rising star in Liberia.

Mariners saw "*the Cape of Palmas*"
    along the West Atlantic charms.
Where dwelt in peace sturdy tribesmen,
    guarding their land 'gainst slave-hunt den.
    O Maryland! Dear Maryland!
    through years kept safe for Liberia.

"*Maryland State* in *Liberia!*"
    The dear old spot once known, for aye.
When Pioneer sires made this their home
    Ere Long, Lone Star bade them welcome.
    O Maryland! Dear Maryland!
    a county blest in Liberia.

Thy rising youths will bless thy name,
    while growing years doth gain thee fame.
Not now "the Cape of Palmas," men praise.
    But statesmen great whom thou dost raise!
    O Maryland! Dear Maryland!
    a burnished light in Liberia.

All praise to God, the Father, Son,
    and Spirit Blest, the Three-in-One
whose guiding hand led fathers well
    to found a home for us to dwell.
    O Maryland! Dear Maryland!
    East Bound'ry line of Liberia.

Land of the Beautiful

REV. FATHER JAMES DAVID KWEE BAKER

How beautiful thy landscapes green
well blessed with gifts at hand!
Thy many falls, and winding rills
present most lovely scene.
Dear land of peace, Liberia aye!
Thy bounds will set men free.
O may thy years, and growth well prove,
thy mission of true love.

Thy coastline broad, and hinterland,
stand rich in oil-palm fields.
Thy mounts and dales, thy lakes, and sounds,
great wealth each does command.
O beauteous land, Liberia aye!
through years thy fame shall spread.
With toil, and learning sound uphold,
thy power still yet untold.

Thy woodlands great, and meadows grand,
with precious ore abound.
Thy boundless meads, thy copious hills,
great hidden wealth command aye!
O, sacred heritage,
thy natural wealth so manifold
will make thy fame most bold.

Thy rivers wide, and oceans deep,
each holds their own blessed gifts.

Thy forests great, and dense grassland,
wild beasts of games they keep.
Land of delight, Liberia aye!
Thy bounds and soil are blessed.
With careful skill thou shalt prevail,
thy greatness men will hail.

Cavalla Grand

REV. FATHER JAMES DAVID KWEE BAKER

An Ode to Cavalla River

Dear Cavalla, broad and hoary,
   O River Grand!
What of thee doth make for glory?
   O River Grand!
Doth thy rapids, spiral flowing,
and thy gurgling waters swelling,
tell the story with full meaning.
   What made thee grand!

Why thy banks stand high and slipp'ry,
   Cavalla Grand !
Why thy mountain-peaks so dreary,
   Cavalla Grand!
Why thy annual floods rise sweeping
when the harvest's ripe for reaping,
why make farmers stare a-weeping,
   O River Grand?

My broad basin doth give bound'ry:
   Liberia aye!
In my spiral flow there's glory:
   Liberia aye!
Each curve marks thine eastern border,
which no alien hand dare alter
while my mountain-peak doth tower,
   O'er Fatherland.

On my slipp'ry slopes there's bounty,
    from days of old.
In my prairies broad there's beauty,
    with wealth untold.
Though men fear my rapids' great flow,
and great floods which lay my banks low,
my rank and strength all doth foreshow
    and make me bold.

With thy wealth and form so hoary,
    O River Grand!
Far and wide will be thy glory,
    O River Grand!
Toil and skill will prove thy great fame,
and by thee our bound'ry fixed name,
though thy whirl be ever the same,
    Cavalla Grand.

Ode to Cape Mount

REV. FATHER JAMES DAVID KWEE BAKER

Great is the joy to see
Cape Mount's beauteous lee
   near Piso Lake.
Rare are her landscape green,
the mountain range and glen!
All hearts by such great scene
   in song awake!

Her dales, and grand high hills,
are blest with springs and rills:
   where Piso stands.
In these, much wealth concealed,
some day to be revealed.
All wants will be relieved,
   near Piso Strand.

Cape Mount was once obscure
until World War made sure
   Piso's great worth.
Aircraft did daily light,
and took off with great flight
to win the World War fight,
   Piso stood forth.

This county gained a fame,
and Liberia's name
    where Piso stands,
no more war ills to fear.
Yet nations will revere
our homes we hold so dear.
    Near Piso strands.

Divine Guidance

REV. FATHER JAMES DAVID KWEE BAKER

O God, the Father, Who doth give
the span of life by which we live,
grant us the grace that we may prove
what wonderous power has Thy sweet love.

O God, the Son, Who by Thy Cross
hath conquered death to gain the loss,
grant us the strength to seek Thy grace
and at the end to see Thy Face.

O God the Spirit by Whose might,
the power of sin is put to flight.
Grant us the light to guide our way
in paths of righteousness each day.

Praise God, the Father, God the Son,
and God, the Spirit, Three in One!
We own Thy sway, Thy love, Thy light
O, Triune God of Glorious might.

Is This Africa

ROLAND TOMBEKAI DEMPSTER

Is this Africa
unfair men once called
Continent of Darkness
Land of baboons, apes, and monkeys
cannibals and men with tails
only fit to be
the servants of other men?

Is this the same Africa
now holding firm her own,
deciding her own fate,
with the sword of faith
fighting her foes
with weapons holier than those
used by the "master-race"?

Is this Africa
in dignity and grace
nowhere surpassed,
in wisdom deep?

Can this be the same Africa,
now center of hope,
of which men once spoke
in vilest terms?

Is this Africa,
Mother Africa

long suppressed, divided,
ruled, impugned?
How proud are we today, Africa,
to note the part, you played
for your sons and daughters
still washed in tears.

Africa's Plea

ROLAND TOMBEKAI DEMPSTER

I am not you—
but you will not
give me a chance,
will not let me be *me*.

"If I were you"—
But you know
I am not you,
yet you will not
let me be *me*.

You meddle, interfere
in my affairs
as if they were yours
and you were me.

You are unfair, unwise,
foolish to think
that I can be you,
talk, act
and think like you.

God made me *me*.
He made you *you*.
For God's sake
let me be *me*.

The Lone Star Shines

ROLAND TOMBEKAI DEMPSTER

The Lone Star is shining
brightly in the dimmest night.
It's shedding its radiant light,
spreading rays like lightning,
clearing the way for others
now held in alien fetters.

The Lone Star, Liberia,
has led the way to freedom,
and quaked many a kingdom
that vaunts its criteria
over all darker faces
as men of lower races.

The Lone Star, how bravely,
it has fought Africa's battle—
It is made an end of struggle,
and shown the world so clearly
that the black man is no fool
that others must always rule.

Shine, shine in the dimmest night,
shed afar thy radiant light
oh, Star of Liberia, vanguard, hero!
Shine, let the world bold see
that God made equal, free.

JULY 14, 1959

When You Die—a Philosophy of Life

ROLAND TOMBEKAI DEMPSTER

It does not matter
how long you live,
how sweet your life,
but when you die,
let it be said:
You eased some burden,
calmed troubled breasts,
did deeds of kindness,
allayed coming storms
for some orphan children,
or those beguiled,
or helped a Christ
to Calvary's rugged hill.
Life is not the thing:
But when you die,
or old or young,
let it be known
you were a human being,
not a cruel, heartless thing,
unmindful of all.
The things that count,
to live or die, is not
the thing that counts:
But when you die,
let people cry
that a friend is gone,
a brother in Christ depart.

The Poet's Ear

ROLAND TOMBEKAI DEMPSTER

The Poet sits alone,
and hears the gibbering spirits
that whisper one by one.
The Poet walks alone,
and hears the squirrels sing,
and the blooming flowers whisper love and beauty.
At dawn of day, the doodoo's song
thus, brings messages all along
to the Poet's ear.
The pepper-bird is heard to say:
"All hail the glorious dawn of day."
The stones and rocks talk in ecstasy
of strength, endurance, and constancy.
Brooklets, day, and night
run in ceaseless flight,
and say the weak of nature so do run.
The great and mighty oceans do forestall
the power of the Mighty God of all.
The bees, the grass and air
talk to the Poet's ear.
Ah, the Poet's ear, marvelous to hear
of the wisdom and the beauty
of Nature's world.

Take the World Away, but Give Me Freedom

ROLAND TOMBEKAI DEMPSTER

Take the world away
with its glories and its honors.
Take what ends today
with the horrors of its stories,
but give me that freedom
that is more than kingdom.

Take all pomp from me
with its emptiness and vaunt.
Drive out empty glee
and all such that do not count,
but give me what I need:
Freedom with all the speed.

Take vain show away,
with all the ills it bears.
Take falsehood today
that dims the sight of seers.
Give me that which the true man has need:
'Tis freedom on which he need must feed.

Give me that freedom,
that is free from serfdom,
that will make me freer
to move, to speak, and then to will,
and never holds my freedom still.

Take away your dukedom:
Suppress not my freedom.
Defile never my manhood
which belongs to my godhood.
'Tis not mine to fling at will
so, to others' urge fulfil.

TUESDAY MORNING, NOVEMBER 8, 1955

Go On and Do, Let the People Talk

ROLAND TOMBEKAI DEMPSTER

I have never seen a nosey place
as this wherein we live.
I've never seen a carefree race
who all their time do give
to foolish things that nothing worth,
but talk and talk and talk.
The busy world that passeth by
is naught to catch their eye.
They know it all, except their own,
what happened here and there.
'Twas done in dark or done alone,
some worthless man 'bout it will talk.
They know your own more than you do,
though they never had the slightest clue.
The thing to do is not to mind
whatever they say or all they do,
but say, "to hell, let the people talk,"
and go and do what you think is right.
For with empty hands and empty hands
they cannot help but while away
their precious time, their only day,
that God doth give but once.

SEPTEMBER 22, 1946

To Man

ROLAND TOMBEKAI DEMPSTER

O little god within undying clay,
supreme, sublime, that sings the ancient lay,
with all his soul, of heroes rare.
Of ancient lore that loudly blare
the godhood in the "man,"'
denounce with frowns the falsehood and the hate
that would invade against the Will of Fate.
Our all and all that would submit to art,
to break the tie and play the "devil's" part,
and bring to naught the godhood in the "man."
Curse all born with lowly minds, depraved,
that dare not seek, or e'er sought or craved
the godhood in the "man."

The Pepper Bird Is Singing

ROLAND TOMBEKAI DEMPSTER

The pepper bird is singing in my ear,
announcing to all that day is broke,
that sleeping Africa may wake to hear
its sweet song that mirth and glee provoke.

The pepper bird is pealing loud its note
of warning to Africans asleep:
To wake up, to wake up, to time devote
to the things that count, no time to weep.

The pepper bird is singing in my ear
telling Africa: Awake, the day
is fleeting fast, the time is passing clear,
the roads by others build, clears the way.

Liberia in Verse and Song

ROLAND TOMBEKAI DEMPSTER

O happy Muse, permit me at this time to sing
this filial song of my nation's birth and rise.
Permit me, yea, that I may longing tribute bring
and to the world, give a bit of a glad surprise.

Ah, loving Muse that knowest well the need of friends,
allow me at this time and date to play the role
that ancient Virgil played to make his means his ends,
and give to Rome its place in history's blazoned scroll.

Ah, make Liberia like Augustan Virgil's Rome
and lend me fire and wit to sing my nation's name,
to raise it as high as to touch the heaven's dome,
and let to the world my nation's worth proclaim.

For thousand years, Liberia free in Africa stood,
land greedy men hailed her, but went without a claim.
God sending each away be fooled in quietude,
they left alone the bliss and took away the blame.

A Sonnet—the Poet's Soul

H. CAREY THOMAS

It is the poet's soul that weeps in silence
o'er a withered rose, that feels a pang of sorrow
when the day is closed. The sighing trees—
the fallen leaf—The murmur of the breeze,
for these, the poet grieves, and in their presence,
all but weeps. He fain would borrow
the Muses harp to soothe his palpitating heart,
and drive away the thoughts that make his feelings smart.
I love the poet's heart, his sympathetic soul—
that soul which looks beyond the veil of tears
and bids me hope and lay aside my fears.
He makes me love the lonely flowers ~ the busy ant,
the frugal bee; he lifts my downcast eyes
and points them to a place among the stars.

Ask Me Why

H. CAREY THOMAS

Ask me why the sun sinks westward—
Why the flickering rays at twilight
fade away from crimson skies.
Ask me why, and I'll tell you
of a soul so sad and lonely—
Pressed with sadness—full of anguish,
looking out with wide despair—
One whose little flame of courage
sinks as sinks the sun at sunset
when the birds are winging home.

Ask me why the wild wind sighing
moans among the plantain trees
why the great expansive ocean,
echoing thru the jungle leaves
fling itself upon the sands,
with ceaseless voices of pain and anguish.
Ask me why, and I will tell you
of the heartaches, heavy like some weighty
Kinjah hanging on the back,
crushing out the dreams of childhood,
pressing down the very soul
till it lingers in repose.

Some say that love is joy and sunshine.
Love is full of merry laughter—
Love is everything divine.
There are pains that love can bring you

which no mortal tongue can tell.
Ask me why, and I can tell you
of the bitter dregs that follow
love's sweet quaff when all is well.

Ask me why the roses wither
why the violets fade and die—
Why the sluggish caterpillar,
tired of its ugly form
leaves behind its loathsome shell.
Ask me why, and I can tell you
as the Roman Poet, Vergil
tells us *Fides tutua non est.*
Faith has vanished from the earth.
Ask me why, and I can tell you.

No Longer Yesterday

H. CAREY THOMAS

We are not swine, but men,
whose passions shaped and fashioned
by a great Divine,
in humble hut destined
or in a thatched shrine,
great kings and princes live.

We are not dogs, but men,
whose dreams and aspirations
reach highest heaven,
e'en though our trails may lead
through steaming swamps
and burning tropic sands.

We are not beasts, but men,
of flesh and blood and soul,
whose changing joys and sorrows—
consuming love and hate—
Fierce passions and great struggles,
are an epic of a race.

We are but men, whose time
and evolution, though
delayed, heap no curses
on the God of Fate—
Nor ask no favors, nor beg
no pity, at the hands
of those whose fortunes rule.

All great and good things come
to them who toil and wait.
The sunset's glow of yesterday
reflects the crimson flush
of dawn—our golden morn.
Today with gladness comes,
no longer yesterday.

Because You Told Me

H. CAREY THOMAS

Because you told me
that rain or sunshine
made no change in you,
that gain, or sometimes
pain with crimson hue,
would never change
your love for me—
Because you told me
that love was like a stream
which flowed forever along
the sunny banks of song.
I picked the roses
and the violets too.
Yea all my worldly goods
I took and laid them
at your gentle feet—
I shut my eyes
to all the many charms around,
and worshipped only you.

In vain, it seems,
this throbbing heart shall beat.
My dripping eyes shall weep,
for though with all
my mortal cares

I have loved throughout the years,
each day it seems
my treasured dream
like vapor melts away.

But even dripping water
wears away the cold hard stone,
and gentle breezes
bend the great stout oak.
Ah, tell me, is my fervent
and devoted love for you
forever lost in passion's woe?

And if some day
when all is lost
and this poor heart
shall cease its feeble taps,
let no useless tears—
No empty sighs—no vacant groans
be shed for me
or heard when I am gone.
For barren gain
and bitter loss in love
are all that is left to me.

When You Sigh

H. CAREY THOMAS

Ah! when you sigh
for me it seems
that clouds come down
and hide the sunshine
in the sky.
For me it seems
that singing birds
and blooming flowers
forget their song
and lose their beauty
for a while.

Yes, Alice Jones
I heard you sigh
one afternoon.
Your little groan
brought to my mind
the distant billows
as they moan
on yonder distant
sandy shores.

For me, a sigh
a groan, a cry
is like a sky
where clouds and shadows
gather for
a storm—and why?
It's when you sigh.

AUGUST 6, 1940

At Sunset

H. CAREY THOMAS

To the Late, Honorable Daniel Edward Howard, Ex-President of Liberia, from 1912–1920.(Commonly known as the War President)

Lonely and sad from the tower he looked
as he waited the ferry-men's call.
His loved ones had crossed, and friends gone before
he alone sat patiently there.

Tired and lonely, and his comrades gone
he alone stood facing the foe.
Sheathing his sword, he patiently waits.
Victorious, our conquering Dan.
A statesman, warrior, churchman, and friend—
Constant, unfailing and true.

Shadows are stealing over the day,
twilight so solemn and gray—
Murmuring voices in the far, far away
beckon the weary one home.

Flowers may fade and wither away;
the perfume still lingers a day.
Temples and statues must crumble and fall
beneath time's hand of decay,
but earth's rarest jewels so precious and few,
eternal shall ever endure.

Those great souls, immortal, who lived not for self
but suffered that others might live,
shall never know death, corrode and decay—
Eternal, shall ever endure.

Echoes of a Longing Heart

H. CAREY THOMAS

Have you seen the shadows creeping
along the edges of the dial?
Have you heard the birdies singing
where the wild deer makes his Jair?
Don't you often think of sighing
when the shades of evening fall,
or do you wonder at the fleeting
of the shadows on the walls?
Does your heart grow wide with longing
for the things you do not see,
and your bosom filled with yearning
for a vision fuller, free?

Hush! hear the distant tom-toms
from the drum of Afric's sons—
Listen to their plaintive folk-song
as it bubbles from their souls.
Ah! those weird, fantastic sounds—
Strains so haunting, sweet, and soft,
tell a story in their song,
echoes of a longing Heart.

Yes, a story, sad and long
of a race that's struggling on,
treading many a path of thorns,
singing, smiling—moves along.

Through the heat of the scorching sun,

sweating—bending to their task—
toiling till the day is done.
What consoles them, you may ask.
Not the thoughts of glorious gain,
nor the hopes of sweet reward,
but the rhythm in their frame—
Music's message to the Bard.

In the eve when twilight falls,
and the moon smiles through the clouds,
listen, you will hear that song,
echoes of a Longing Heart.

The Tom-Toms Beat No More

H. CAREY THOMAS

The warning drums,
the Jungle's never-failing wireless
no longer beats upon the hills.
The warning cry,
the plaintive note,
is hushed among the Jungle leaves.

Where are the drums,
the great bass drums
our Fathers made of stout deer skins,
whose rousing echoes
woke the slumbering warrior,
and bade him seize
his spear with haste?

Where are the drums,
those ancient drums
that moved the very hearts of cowards
to meet the foe
unflinching?

Where are the drums,
those mighty drums
that warned the tribesmen far and near
lest dangerous foes assail them
unawares?
The tom-toms beat no longer.

It cannot be
that those stout arms
that beat the taps
unerringly
have tired of their vigilance.

It cannot be
that pale men's lips have uttered charms,
so powerful,
given gifts
so glittering
to still that passion
for that land
where our fathers' bones are laid.

Take up the drums,
the great bass drums,
those ancient drums.
Come, beat the taps
let tribesmen distant,
tribesmen near
be warned.
That pale-faced strangers
with unhallowed feet
profane this heritage our fathers gave.

Ebony Dust

BAI T. MOORE

In this speck of ebony dust
blown over east and western climes
forever burns the yearning
to tap the springs of ancient bards
whose tales of African heroes
lie buried in the ruins
of the kingdoms that are hidden
beneath the waste of centuries.
Empires like Bornu, Songhay and Malinke
or the domains of the Bantu.
Fabulous tales of elegant courts
trimmed in royal splendor
at Jene and Timbuktu,
where kings and comely queens
surrounded by their courtiers
kept aflame ambitions
and millions on the march.
Tales of brilliant warriors,
on galloping steeds and camels
who wield the sword and left
behind in blood and flames,
achievements of the scholars
who gave the world the rudiments
of medicine, math, and arts,
and the secrets of the stars.
To catch the souls of mockingbirds
whose lives and loves enrich
the boat songs of the Congo.

The Niger, and the Nile,
or the new "High Life" of Ghana.
To carve with pen like masters
whose delicate hands create
a ritual dancing mask,
or a silent god in ebony.

Monrovia Market Women

BAI T. MOORE

the Monrovia
market women
they are something-o
'foreday in the morning
   the pepper birds
   dog
   goats and
   chickens
chase them
out of bed and
send them running
like red ants
on nettles
they grab old
squeaking buckets
run to hydrants
ch-u-u-u-u-u
and duck in
foul enclosures
smelling with pee
throw cold water
on they
back
belly
and between they legs
and all
they snatch
young crying babies

tie them snugly
on they back
shove fat tits
in they mouth
to hush them up
then rush by
    foot
    bus or
    taxi
to the arteries
pumping life
into the markets
of Monrovia
they rush to
buying depots
    Tubman Bridge
    Duala
    Belema (for Mesu Fish)
    Juakpebli (near USAID/RL)
    and Oldest Kongotown
to stop the trucks and pickups
fluff of zoba bags of
    cassadas
    potatoes
    plawa sauce leaves and
    dry meat like
        wild bushgoat
        boa constrictor
        elephant skin
        nyangaboy
and other fuyu fuyu
these women must have strong backs
and legs and hands to push and fight
and hold on to their market money

wrapped in a belt of country cloth
which they tie around the waist
but wait now the fun begins in
market stalls where chattering
and palavering (like a colony of rice birds)
and dollar notes and coins commence
passing the confusion through
a hundred thousand fingers
   come good friend
   buy my part me
   I go dash you
goes on endlessly till dusk.

Africa in Retrospect

Africa
a paradox
or is it?
in Lisbon
in a dank room
a cartographer sits
he splashes black
ink on Africa
and they call her
"the dark continent."

Africa
imagination people her
with pig meat
eating cannibals
and fire eating
savages, who live
on human sacrifices.

Africa
explorers rush to
her, and carry
back to Europe,
news of gold
and diamonds,
elephant tusks

and spices, ready
to be carted off
to Europe, and
the boys in
Fleet Street
struck it rich.

Africa
but the place
is the white man's
grave, full of
snakes and pagan
savages, the jungle
inaccessible—
to hell with
all of that,
light is all
Africa needs—
they dump in
rum and Bibles
and light up
the god damn place.

Africa
what a big
bonanza,
everything come
running there, a
happy dumping ground;
from big time
operators, garbed in
boots and helmets,

the famed French
Foreign Legion, to
renegades from every
corner of the world.
armed with flags
and cannons, some
come by sailing
vessels, others brave
the caravans across
the great Sahara,
just to get to
Africa, to civilize
the Natives.

The Legend of Shad Tubman

BAI T. MOORE

The scribes wrote a name
when the mother's pains subsided
and that name became Shad Tubman.

Shad Tubman Tubman Tubman
is a household word
around the world
which grew up from a legend.
Somewhere down in Gbenelu
where oldsters still recall
Shad the poor man's friend and lawyer.
Out of humble depths he rose
passing sieves which tutored him
never to lose the common touch
which has raised him high above
all contemporary leaders.
His ready grasp
and warm handshake
his winning smiles
are genuinely bestowed
upon all he meets from day to day.
Despite the ceaseless grind
which a Head of State must bear,
he has only once to meet you
in the milling crowd before him
and your name and face are fixed
among thousands he can call at sight.
Shad Tubman is a household name
which grew up from a legend
somewhere down in Gbenelu.

A Wingless Bird

BAI T. MOORE

For Buster C.

He woke up
in the early dawn
obsessed with dreams to soar
to soar as high as heaven
or as high as heaven
would let him go.

Full of hope
he looked up
in the wide blue sky
with anxious eyes
to see how high to set his goal.

His golden wings were clipped
and the melody in his voice
and his silver flute
were plucked from him
to rot
in the Firestone Plantations.

My Africa

BAI T. MOORE

Where do pepper birds tell of dawn
and tribesmen hasten to the swamp
to drink the palm wine bubbling with
the beetles and the squirming worms?
And spiked with leaves and *seejohn* roots
which bring the aged youth.
Where women pound their daily morsels
in mortars fashioned out of wood
or drain the tiny brooks and creeks
with dip nets made from palm leaf twine
in search of fish and crabs.
Where cunning beasts and insects
roam around the jungles
trying to dodge the spear and arrows
dipped in poison cooked from nuts and leaves.
Where witch men make lightning strike
an enemy or an innocent tree,
or humans change to snakes and cows
that bullets never kill;
Where *Polo* men can span the *Tuma*
in the night with vines and twigs,
a swinging monkey bridge, which
is just as strong as steel.
Where genii dwell in groves and streams
and offer wealth and fame to those
who dare to keep their laws or die.
Where death is just another step
to join the unseen spirit world,

and Muslim and the Christian prophets
tell the pagan of a heaven
shining with unheard of gems
high above the jungles,
free of all which ache the soul.
Where daring feats of warriors gone
and powerful kings with mighty harems
are reckoned now in caves and stones
or handed down in fairy tales?
Where else but the land of pepper birds?

The Bulldozer

BAI T. MOORE

you strain and grunt
you puff and blow
you chew up concrete walls
and knock down mango trees
you chew-chew and chew
but your belly's never full
in your ugly jaws you chew
all our homes of Congo mats
you chew up all the market stalls
and leave our wives with harried nights
you chew up all our crowded dens
and hush our high-life music
we stand in awe
and watch the scene in apathy
we are the squatters
we are the lot
who keep forever wandering
looking for a piece of land
that we can call our home

The Hallelujah Stuff

BAI T. MOORE

Say, good friend in the long white gown,
with darkened specks and bushy hair
looking like the country devil, yelling,
"Hallelujah! Come to Jesus all you people,
Uncle Sam got plenty dough
for everyone to have his share,
but money na' hand and back na' ground,
so, help me, hallelujah!"
Whence come this hallelujah stuff,
this ranting in the streets?
You know it's not an African myth,
where tribesmen worship stones and trees.
Who can't see 'neath your holy gown,
the juju bags and bush goat horns,
stuffed with white shells beaded
in a field of red and black,
that you wear to bring you luck?
I fear your faith in these, my friend
will make you miss the pearly gates,
when Peter calls the mighty roll,
the roll of those condemned to hell
and those who are bound for heaven.
The gazing flock that pass you by
are going down to Waterside
to buy their rice and palm oil,
and are wiser than you think.
They want to see a fleshy racket
full of jazz and *Samgba*.

You know just what I mean,
a team of naked women—
zooting silk and G-strings,
something with a fleshy touch
that gets one feeling happy.
That's the racket with the dough
and not the hallelujah kind.

Say, tell me where you got this stuff
you peddle round the streets
with the image of the cross and plate
blaspheming what the good Book said?
Mind you, hell is boiling over
with hobos trying to make the grade
with just this hocus-pocus crap.
If you but knew you head the list
of those who are bound for hell,
you'd quit the rant and clear the streets
with all that hallelujah bunk.

Yana Boys

BAI T. MOORE

Yana Jews of Water Street
dotting here and yonder
and weighted down with *Fanti* prints,
nylon slips and easy wares,
cheap perfumes and mambo rings
shining bright like gold—
How fare you thru the maize and squeeze
made fast by long established hands?
Is it the genuine smile you wear
with sparkling snow-white teeth,
or your swiftness like a barking deer,
or sugar-coated tongue, *baa*
which offers you a chance
to eke a simple livelihood.
Or are you getting ripe in age
to reckon loss and gain
instead of bartering rice and meat,
palm oil, snuff, and condiments
among expanded families
in crowded village quarters?
I tell you *Yana boys*,
your mobile line is taking root
no matter who you touch.
With the constant change in fashions
to suit your gazing customers
your chance is here to stay.

The Strength of a Nation

BAI T. MOORE

The nation cannot rise above
the pains of common masses
whose devotion and the country's love
is rooted in the simple homes
of bamboo mats and mud
roofed with grass and raffia palm.
The rich black dirt entwined with streams
that nourish paddy fields with crops
which offer tho what scanty means
will keep the hearth aglow.
The rich who kick the dust and flee
when circumstances pinch the pride
may go where wealth can make them free,
but not that humble wretch who stays
and tills the soil from dawn to dusk
throughout his humble days.
I mean the man who loves the land
who worries when the trouble clouds
are blowing over his country,
and who with a willing heart and hand
will share his burden for the flag,
the strength of the nation lies with him.

Ko Bomi hee m koa

Gola

> koa mu wo yeye
> o hinya kpo goo mbe
> ko Bomi hee m koa
> ko mi nyinia kei ma
> ma jeima wuye m zoo

English

> go tell mother
> to bring my root pot
> to Bomi. I'm going
> where I'll do my stuff
> and sweat it out hard

Gola

> koa mu wo dada
> o hinya kpo goo mbe
> ko Bomi hee m koa
> ko mi nyinia kei ma
> ma jeima wuye m zoo

English

> go tell father
> to bring my root pot
> to Bomi. I'm going
> where I'll do my stuff
> and sweat it out hard

Gola

>koa mu wo Siafa
>o hinya duaze n noo
>ko Bomi hee m koa
>ko mi nyinia kei ma
>ma jeima wuye m zoo

English

>go tell Siafa
>to bring his *duazet*
>to Bomi. I'm going
>where I'll do my stuff
>and sweat it out hard

Gola

>koa mu wo Mambu
>o wande gongoeh
>ko Bomi hee m koa
>ko mi nyinia kei ma
>ma jeima wuye m zoo

English

>go tell Mambu
>to stop his worrying
>to Bomi. I'm going
>where I'll do my stuff
>and sweat it out hard

Gola

>koa mu jamba
>o wande deve eh
>ko Bomi hee m koa
>ko mi nyinia kei ma
>ma jeima wuye m zoo

English
> tell my jamba
> to cease advising
> to Bomi. I'm going
> where I'll do my stuff
> and sweat it out hard

Ba nya m go koma

BAI T. MOORE

Gola

> ba nya m go koma o
> e koma je jee
> ba nya m go koma o
> m jei yei
>
> mfe goye joa nyu ndo
> ba nya m go koma o
> ekoma je jee
> ba nya m go koma o
> m jei yei

THEY SAID I DID NOT BORN

English

> they said I did not born
> to have a child is painful
> they said I had no child
> so, I will sit down so
>
> I will rear nobody's child
> they said I had no child
> to have a child is painful
> they said I had no child
> so I will sit down so

Dear Patrice Lumumba

KONA KHASU (JAMES ROBERTS)

Like a cotton tree
withers before its bloom
a tough of flame
rudely hushed by the furious storm
your small but bright flame.
O Lumumba,
perhaps you lie so low
so cold,
smiling, joyously for that flame
the flame you willed to us.

Perhaps
you giggled innocently
like you always did
with thoughts, escorting each smile
each giggle, or,
perhaps
you lay so crushed, fossilized
by the cold earth,
and your thoughts germinate,
sprout, and shoot up

in the lands of our Africa.
O Lumumba,
so selfless, so innocent
yet so guilty, you spent your life
in some unknown place

brutalized,
mutilated,
like thousands of soldiers
before life was hastily plucked out of you,
the lights put out

where lays your grave now,
decorated by the trees you loved so well.
Covered by the very sun that
ushered in that day
that fateful day that saw you fall,
never to rise again.

O Lumumba,
hear your brother shout your name,
you, little light
threatened by this great sun,
born of lowly parents
born to bring us light
to give us our rights.
We hear the tom-toms of our drums
we feel the rhythm
of our marching soldiers
we smell the sweat
of our struggling brother,
we see mothers, exhorting
their brave sons to war.

They fear no death.
They cannot die.
They cannot die.
The struggle is one.
The time is here.

We cannot wait.
We cannot wait.
We cannot wait.
We must not wait.
We must not wait.
Your flame draws us
onward to the fight.

Our Man on Broad Street

KONA KHASU (JAMES ROBERTS)

He came down Broad Street
ninety degrees temperature
humidity eighty
he was sweating
profusely, but
he wore a grey flannel suit
a three-piece flannel suit,
vest
coat
and pants,
all evidence of his civilization.
On his head sat a hat.
You could see
he was hot.
But he could not wear
his loose,
cool shirt
made of thin-out cotton
suitable for his oven-hot climate
no,
not this time,
this place
he was going for an interview
he had to wear his civilization
   on his back
   on his head
   and on his arse
he was civilized

his dress showed it.
At the intersection of Broad and Center Streets
he met a strangely garbed man
resplendent in his colorful robe
the stranger said
he was from Ashanti
the other fellow,
our European-dressed friend
speaking in muffled words
like the talk of the dumb,
accused the stranger of plotting
to turn Liberia into the Jungle City.
"Your costume is too bright"
he grunted
"Your hair too thick
not brushed.
Your pants
which look like
stringed together ropes
are like the Liberian zebra."
The stranger slowly turned
and in a polite
gentle smile
retorted in a brilliant Oxford accent:
"Pardon, sir
could you show me where the library is?
I'd like also to know where the museum is.
You see
sir
I am a visitor
I'd also like to spend the night
at the theatre."
And when our European-dressed friend
turned to leave,

the stranger pled:
"One moment
sir,
where is the city park?"
Our civilization-coated friend
stared in confusion,
in utter amazement.
He had never heard of these things before.
A brief moment of thought dragged itself out.
He recollected himself and said,
"The library you'll find
at every street corner
it has signs
they say
'Do not order your drinks until you ask the price,'
oh yes,
the bartenders are out to cheat
as for the park
each street is a park
you have to be careful of the traffic.
Bonds for motor accidents come quite cheaply,
a dollar and fifty cents only."
After much thought,
"You're in the theatre district already."
The poor stranger crunched his teeth,
tightened his body muscles,
fluids flowing instantaneously
fortified to receive the shock.
"Over yonder is playing, 'Cowboys and Indians.'
Here, 'What's doing, Pussy Cat,'
the corner theatre has 'Spartacus' Great Deeds.'"
"I see, my friend,"
the quiet stranger said,
"I think I've just decided

I'll pass the night
in my room
reading Wole Soyinka
thanks anyway
Ol' boy."

NOVEMBER 13, 1966, FIAMA, MONROVIA

Unnamed Thing

KONA KHASU (JAMES ROBERTS)

My toe knocks the rock
I stop to talk
to it
I pour my drink
on the ground
my mother drinks with me!
slowly
the rock assumes a shape
see the eyes
mouth
ears
it says something to me
it speaks to me
listen to the rock
remembrances of our hurts
a thousand years old
ooze out of the rock
and it pains!

OCTOBER 28, 1965

Their Words—Deception

KONA KHASU (JAMES ROBERTS)

They say we must wait
wait, son, wait your turn
education is the only key to success,
so, study hard
study hard, son, study hard
study damned hard to fill the places of your leaders
they tell us to work hard
plant farms, son, plant farms
they tell us many things
they tell us

what they tell us is too much
they say we are free
the freest country in the world
they tell us we are democratic
the most democratic nation in the world
they say they had an election here
tell us that Tubman was returned

they tell us we are rich for this,
rich son, you are rich,
they say all will be well and prosperous
for another four years
Tubman will spend 1,000,000 a year
on his health
and that will make us the healthiest nation on earth

they tell us we are progressing
the returned president will continue the progress
we are strong, they say
the strongest country in the world
they tell us the world looks at us
the most looked at country in the world
they tell us the world respects us
the most respected nation on earth
they tell us many things

they tell us we are great
the greatest nation on earth
don't you feel your greatness
we are cultured
the most cultured nation in the world
the saddest people who are also the happiest people
in the world they tell us jokes
they say we must laugh
sometimes we do not want to laugh
some people laugh
not loud, though
some people cry

everybody does something
because there is nothing to do
so, we listen to jokes
we demand more rice
but all we get is jokes, jokes
only jokes are given to us
so, we demand more jokes
only jokes can sooth our hurt
only jokes can ease our pain

because it is only jokes that we can get
we know only jokes

jokes we have heard all our lives
jokes we have had all our lives
then someone tells us the truth
we laugh at him
because they say we must laugh at him
now we are a laughing nation
laughing and being laughed at
because we have lived with many things
we have heard so much
we have seen so much
we have known so much
too much not to laugh
really too much not to laugh.

But one day Liberia
will have to stop laughing.
Liberia will have to take account of its century-plus age.
It will be funny then, no jokes.
the results will be startlingly frightening.

To Time Our Enemy

KONA KHASU (JAMES ROBERTS)

Speedily we grow old
resolutions upon resolutions
resolutions made
resolutions of resolutions made
deeds done to undo
time presses on us all
takes our hands and wrinkles them
takes hold of our feet
makes them immobile
takes away our motion, our push
time, our constant, ever present enemy
takes hold of our faces
renders them invisible, unrecognizable
gradually, no quickly
we are washed away into the grey, bleak shades
the unforgotten
all our resolutions
come to memories
resolute thoughts and actions of impotency
rested in the minds of men
never, never made to speak and walk.

MARCH 18, 1969

The Old Stream

KONA KHASU (JAMES ROBERTS)

Rays of sunlight streaming bright
blinding strokes
strike the stream
the stream speaks
it lives
it provides our needs
our ancestors are in it
the stream runs
it visits
the stream carries messages
from village to village
our ancestors sent greetings
our fathers are not dead
they are searching
searching for life
the life after life
our fathers are not dead
they are for life
o stream of ancient power
your powers are not lost
our fathers' canoe
rode gallantly
on your watery surface
they went to war
to feasts
to fish
to collect the harvest
up and down stream

towards the sun
no longer do our canoes
rest upon your glassy body
no longer do our fathers
ride your calm surface
our canoes are
resting now
your surface is resting
it is resting
they form a link
between our fathers and us
a link
though strained
never breaks.

PART III

Contemporary Liberian
Poetry, 1990–Present

PART III

Who's on Watch?

ALTHEA ROMEO-MARK

Our watchman stands guard in his dreams.
It is there he keeps thieves at bay.

They strike at 3:00 a.m.
when rain is a dull beat on rooftops
that puts all but robbers to sleep.

Before the watchman dozes and dreams,
he beats and rattles an empty drum,
scrapes his cutlass along metal gates
and windows, wrought iron bars,
to sound his dedication to our defense.

But thieves in the bush are also committed
and strike when the rain is most hypnotic.

In our wee morning stupor,
we dream of bandits
capturing the python
that steals eggs and chicken
from our coop.

But it's the geese that
have been quietly smuggled away,
gone when we and the watchman wake.

Were the honking creatures sedated, too,
by the seductive rhythm of rain?

Only the moon truly monitors,
knows the secrets of bandits,
knows the key to stealing noisy geese.

Visiting Khufu

ALTHEA ROMEO-MARK

Not getting younger in age, I decide to be brave, "walk the walk."
It is Cairo and who does not want to see the pyramids?
We are here for the day to take in BC history
in its sand-dusted surroundings.

We are forbidden to climb sacred surfaces,
but my granddaughter cannot resist clambering
up the ancient stones to pose before a guard waves a warning.

At the entrance to the tallest pyramid
we see sweat-beaded tourists spilling out.
The climb demands the agility of goats.
And here I am, not nimble.
I challenge the years I have lived,
put all three scores and ten to the test.

We, from different lands, a sampling of generations, stoop at the
    entrance.
My daughter, my bolster, behind me,
we continue arching our backs up the dim-lit path.

Well-spaced wooden steps prevent slipping and sliding.
Bannisters on each side support our bending walk.
Sweat dampens our forehead. As we climb,
I convince myself it is a once a lifetime thing never to be done again.

And finally, we reach Pharaoh Khufu's tomb.
I glimpse my goat-footed granddaughter
and godmother patiently waiting.

Khufu's not at home, long ago taken away for safety,
for the preservation of Egypt's history,
secured from the hand of tomb raiders
selling ancient history to the highest bidder.

I am proud as Khufu is to be Pharaoh.
Hot and weak-kneed I feel as if I have conquered Mount Everest,
not something on my bucket list.
I am not one to die for fame. This climb was enough.

Oya (Wind in Cape Town)

ALTHEA ROMEO-MARK

The trees bend, point left.
This is the way they say
with their branches.

The wind-goddess dictates.
Those crossing her path
must hold tightly onto themselves
and their possessions.

The punishment for
disobeying her orders,
GO LEFT,
is the stripping of your dignity.

Oya threatens
to dislodge your grip on safety,
throw you to the ground,
strip you of your clothing,
steal your hat, pluck your hair-piece,
snatch knots, bandeaux,
pull at your earrings,
battle you for your handbag.

Do not resist her bullying.
The mighty trees
have succumbed to her will.
Who are you to disobey?
So, go left when she tells you to.

A Different Kind of Pied Piper 2020

ALTHEA ROMEO-MARK

It arrived. We did not see it cross the 2019 border.
We did not hear its whistle like a creeping hurricane.
It did not come with drumming rain nor sliding hurtling mud.
It didn't rattle or shake like an earthquake.
Nor was it a spinning, crushing cone,
gobbling up and spitting out homes.
It didn't spit fire, didn't spew swallowing ash.
Neither was it the creeping grey mist in a film of doom.
It did not shout the bloody cries of war
nor arrived in any of nature's devastating costumes.

It sent its unseen army out not just to scout.
But chose those who could not resist its call.
They fell in line behind it.

Many felt its hellish whip that left them racked in pain.
Phlegm filled up throats like a clogged moat.

Its victims remain secluded while it stole their breath.
And countless followed the invisible Pied Piper of death.

The Cat-Gods Have Fallen

ALTHEA ROMEO-MARK

Cairo cats surround us.
Not all are unblemished.
Many are skittish bags of bones.
Beauty alone cannot save
the homeless hustlers
roaming the dusty streets.

Some are artful dodgers,
their "nine lives" put to the test
during their daily darting
between speeding cars.

When not poking
around rubbish heaps,
cats seek refuge
under abandoned cars,
peep out hopefully
at big-hearted passers-by
who have more than
an affectionate pat
in their generous hands.

Cairo and cats run side by side.
We cannot see one without the other.
We pass them on the stairways,
spy them under restaurants tables,

watch them dash down alleyways,
sprint across the courtyards
of mosque and museums.

Cats, you were once
revered as goddesses,
buried with your owners,
seen as protectors of pharaohs.
Oh, how low you have fallen.

Praise Song for My Children

PATRICIA JABBEH WESLEY

Let me be your *Mami Wata*, your River Gee,
crossing you into old Grebo country,
after the hills give way, after the truck slides through
mud and rocks, through dangerous muddy ditches
along Zwedru's lost forest
in search of our fathers' homelands.

Let me be your Mama Africa, your Mama
that grew out of old streams of old rivers
from Kehlebo to Karlorkeh, all the way to Tugbakeh.
Where after so long, only small roosters
remain in a town that used to be ours.

Let me come to you at dawn, my children,
my calabash, wet from the early dawn's
water-fetching-run, my *lappa*, wet from the brush,
from the cry of old pepper birds,
the owl's howling, from the old footpaths lost
to the wanderer's feet.
Let me come to you bearing tears on my face
after the war, after the villages have crumbled
under the weight of grave hate.

Let me be your landfill, your garbage dump,
the one, only who could carry you in her young,
suppled womb, carrying you with my youth,
carrying you, even though Liberia was losing
herself, and from afar, we could see

the oncoming smoke of war.
Let me come to you, bearing palm branches
that weathered too quickly in the heat of March.
Here, take from my hand, and drink, my child,
one by one, take and drink.
After the afterbirths have parched hard
in the soil where we did not bury them.
After our feet have become parched from running,
after our way back home has been burned by war,
let me be your *Mami Wata*,
your Mama, rising out of the wild ocean tide.
Let me be your consolation
that the land I gave to you is dying.

I am becoming an old woman, now, my sons.
I am becoming my mother and her mother's mother.
I am becoming the ghosts of my mothers.
I am becoming *Iyeeh*, bowlegged,
I am becoming fire and rain.
I am becoming *Sebo*.
I am becoming the water-bearer.
I am becoming the calabash
that was not shattered in the shattering.

Let me sing to you, my daughters, you who have
never known where we come from.
You who will never know your mother's tongue,
you who have become the metaphor of lost
warriors, who were captured by war.
Let me be your songwriter, the song you sing,
the dirge you do not know how to sing.

Let me wrap around you, my *lappa* that has been
lost in the storm. Let me lay down

all my *lappas* for you to walk on,
my blood-soiled *lappas* from the war.
Let me come to you, my daughters, when the sun
becomes yellow and then red, when it seems
the sun is falling down upon us.

Let me come to you, carrying the moon
in my warm palms. Let me be your *Mami Wata*,
your one Mama, rising out of the waves of war.
Let me be your road map home.
Let us walk together homeward, where the ocean
roars in peace and in war, the rising tides
along Liberia's coast.
Let me be your tears.
Let me be the Mesurado.

When I rise at dawn, my children, I long for you,
but I long for home more.
I long for a lost country that I seek to know again.
When I rise, my sons, I long for the sound of the drum
that used to sit at *Tuwah-Kai*.
I long for cassava shoots and for the banana tree
to bloom again. I long for me.
I long for the girl that was lost.
I long to find my feet again, to find my feet again
to find my feet again.

I long to be me.
Let me come to you, carrying hope in my hands.
Let me come to you, carrying hope in my hands.
Let me come to you, my daughters,
carrying hope in my hands.

November 12, 2015

PATRICIA JABBEH WESLEY

For Liberia

November 12, thirty years after our failed coup,
and I am driving through another city.
Hills, valleys, old houses clinging to years gone.

I've been an alien so long,
sometimes I feel like belonging.

But the ground here is gray, soft, clay rocks
in between white soil, clay enough to turn soil
into pots and plates into jugs.

Difference is measured not only in the cold
November frost, the falling leaves
or in the slow yellowing of oak
even though we know that no matter
how long it takes the oak

to yellow and turn red like fire, red like blood,
no matter how stubborn its will,
the oak will shed its leaves like
all the other trees, become as brittle
as dry limbs after a forest fire.

November 12, and my mind takes me way back home.
Home, the humid sun, bright, hot, like fire,

and the town, divided by the ocean
and the river, the past of bloodshed,

the burning anger and pain, when years
ago, a hero came, or shall
we call him coward? Thomas Quiwonkpa,

coup planner or shall we call him the messenger
of death, sent by alien people
to rob us of home? Liberia, fire, death,
the massacre of our people, the beginning
of the rest of our lives in exile.

November 12, as I drive through this strange town,
where for years, my heart has longed for home,
the early morning mist, rising out of the Mesurado,
the honking cars, the market women on their way
to work, and out of nowhere, my neighbors'
voices, shouting at another hard day.

November 12, but this is where a road leads home,
the earth, red, blood and water, my family line

where the soil still holds onto my umbilical cord,
buried in the hills of Dolokeh, home, and Monrovia,
where my father's grave awaits my return
so I can kneel and cry and pray, and tell him how
sometimes, I am so lonely in this far away country,
I want to walk and walk and walk and walk
and walk until I'm back home again.

November 12, no matter how ugly they say home looks,
there's never a day when you do not want to go back home.

What Took Us to War

Every so often, you find
a piece of furniture, an old head wrap
or something like a skirt
held together by a rusty pin.
Our years, spilled all over the ruggedness
of this war-torn place,
our years, wasted like grains of rice.

Relics of your past, left for you,
in case you returned accidentally
or intentionally, in case you did not
perish with everyone else.
Something hanging onto thread,
holding onto the years
to be picked up, after locusts
and termites have had their say,
the graciousness of looters,

the graciousness of termites
and temporary owners of a home
you built during your youth,
during the Samuel Doe years
when finding food was your life goal.
How gracious, the war years,
how gracious, the warlords,
their fiery tongues and missiles.

All the massacres we denied,
and here we are today, coming upon
a woodwork of pieces of decayed
people that are not really pieces
of woodwork at all.
This should be an antique, a piece
of the past that refused to die.

Wood does not easily rot, but here,
termites have taken over Congo Town
the way Charles Taylor claimed the place,
the way Charles Taylor claimed
our land and the hearts of hurting people,
the way the Atlantic in its wild roaming
has eaten its way into town
even as we roamed, in search of refuge,

the way whole buildings have crumbled
into the sea, the way the years
have collapsed upon years.
What took us to war has again begun,
and what took us to war
has opened its wide mouth
again to confuse us.
What took us to war, oh, my people!

When Monrovia Rises

PATRICIA JABBEH WESLEY

The city is not a crippled woman at all. This city
is not a blind man at a potholed roadside, his

cane, longer than his eye, waiting for coins to fall
into his bowl, in a land where all the coins were lost

at war. When Monrovia rises, the city rises with
a bang, and I, throwing off my damp beddings,

wake up with a soft prayer on my lips. Even God
in the Heavens knows how fragile this place is.

This city is not an egg or it would have long
emerged from its shell, a small fiery woman

with the legs of snakes. All day, boys, younger
than history can remember, shout at one another

on a street corner near me about a country they
have never seen. Girls wearing old t-shirts speak

a new language, a corruption by that same ugly war.
You see, they have never seen better times.

Everyone here barricades themselves behind steel
doors, steel bars, and those who can afford also

have walls this high. Here, we're all afraid that one

of us may light a match and start the fire again

or maybe one among us may break into our home
and slash us all up not for our wealth, but for

the memories they still carry under angry eyelids.
Maybe God will come down one day without his boots.

Maybe someone will someday convince us that after
all the city was leveled, we are all the same after all,

same mother, same father, same root, same country,
all of us, branches and limbs of the same oak.

I Want to Be the Woman

PATRICIA JABBEH WESLEY

I don't want to be the other woman.
Don't want to stay up nights
for the phone call.
Take your excuses and pour them
down some rusty drain
as from a wine bottle,
and kill yourself at dawn.

I want to stay the woman who stands
there, waiting,
so her husband's lies rest like dust
on the windshield of an old car.
I want to carry deep scars
of brokenness all my life,
like our mothers' mothers' mothers,
who did not learn how to kill
that old African polygamy,
but killed it anyway.

I am The Woman, the maker of the bed,
the unused love keeper, the breeder
of fine children, scarred
only by broken dreams in the broken places,
where our foremothers found company
with other women, and buried
their babies' naval strings with hopes
that someday, something would happen.
No, I am already The Woman,

Khade-Wheh, headwife,
the home-keeper, *Khade*, the owner
of the afterbirth and the afterbirth pains,

Khade-Wheh, the holder of hot pots,
the keeper of the homestead,
the fireplace holder,
the powerless, powerful African woman,
after the old paths
of lonely women, betrothed
too early to unknown, ugly men.
No, I am not looking for love.
This body is too old
for lovers to hang out in my dreams
or in my daydreaming.

Don't lie to me. I am too beautiful for you.
Don't fool yourself. I do not need love.
I do not think my *Iyeeh* knew love,
and I used to hear her say
that love could not make a farm.
My *Iyeeh*, whose bare feet
grew thorns from walking back
and forth from farm to farm homestead,
from farm to town, from tilling the land
like a husbandless wife,

my *Iyeeh*, who entertained all
the small wives of an already blind husband,
my *Bai*, who was not too blind
to sleep with multiple wives,
but *Iyeeh* had only one husband despite
the crowd of wives
populating her marriage.

Yes, I want to be the villain
only to my husband. I want to ground
my last years under a cold blanket,
to guard my woman part
from your invasion.
I want to greet my ancestors, our mothers,
with this old piece of my brokenness.
Yes, I am *Khade-Wheh*,
the mother of mothers.

Biography When the Wanderers Come Home

PATRICIA JABBEH WESLEY

This is where we were born,
in these corrugated rugged places,
where boys chasing girls chasing
boys chasing other girls chasing bellies
chasing babies chasing other babies
chasing poverty, chased death.
Of potholed streets and bars and sex
and other girls, getting drowned
forever and ever in loveless love.
And then the fires of our lives
lit other fires of other lives
with lust and then
there was no longer us.
So then the war came with its bullets,
chasing people chasing the bombs,
and ghost towns sprang up
with carcasses of the dying
and the dead. And like mushrooms,
the dead rose up to claim the land
and we were no more.
But the fires still burned in the wombs
and in the eyes of the city streets
below which the dead lovers and
love lie. And there was life again
out of so much pain,
and life took on its own life again
and the girls returned on the backs
of surreal horses in search

of that old fire. But these were no longer
the same girls or boys or men or women.
But this is where we grew up, on these
sidewalk streets, in these rugged places.
This is where the streets come in.
This is where we belong.
This is where life begins.

We Departed Our Homelands and We Came

PATRICIA JABBEH WESLEY

—Grebo Saying

We departed our homelands and we came,
so the Grebo say, we came with our hands
and we came with our machetes

so we too, could carve up the new land.

When we left home, we crossed streams
and we climbed up hills; we set out through
wet brushes, and the rivers parted
so we could cross.

We know that if the leopard should leap,
it is because it sees an antelope passing.

We came, not so we could sit and watch
a wrestling match, not so we could watch
the land on which our feet walk,
rise beyond our reach.

We journeyed from our homelands,
and we came, so, let it be known *that we left*
our homelands, and we came.

When we arrived, we dug up the earth,
and in this new earth, we laid down
our umbilical cords, forever.

So let it be known among the people, *we left
all the beauty of our homelands* not so

we would sit out on *The Mat* to wail.

An Elegy for the St. Peter's Church Massacre

PATRICIA JABBEH WESLEY

I fled the war in that first ceasefire.
Missing all the other wars, the other massacres,
the burning and re-burning of Monrovia,

the silencing again of those who had already
been silenced in that first sweep.
My neighbors envied me through dark eyelashes,
skeletal cheekbones and hunger.

I envy those who were massacred.
Those who never saw their killers approach
with heavy boot steps that made no sound
in the dark morning hours.

Those who died in colonies, in one huge group
at the *President's* order.
They arrived in death, holding hands—
mothers, hugging their babies, men,
helping their wives over the hills of death;
talking, laughing, singing,
they walked happily in death.

It is such a good thing to go with company.

The Atlantic's wailing winds at the hurried steps
of hundreds of soldier boots
will live forever with the living.

I honor those who were massacred
at St. Peter's Lutheran by troops
with only an errand to run.
The raining of guns upon sleeping people
as if this were not already July.

How I envy those who never heard those
stalking boot steps at the church doors that night;
never saw the faces of their murderers,
never had to count the hours remaining—
only one shot, and it was all over.

When we wept with Glayee, who arrived
clinging to two toddler girls at Soul Clinic
Refugee Camp, how could I envy her?
Haunted eyes, scarred arms and legs from
climbing up that barbed-wire fence, a slash wrist
for where they spilled her own blood
in sacrificial offering.

It is a sad story when we survive the massacre
of hundreds who were only sleeping before God.
It is a sad story when one survives
the massacre of the whole world like that.

They Want to Rise Up

PATRICIA JABBEH WESLEY

In the unknown hours, when daylight is coming in,
and the dark gathers for departure,
when the winds stir pebbles along Liberia's shores,
you can hear the wailing.
From the coast of Harper to Sinoe, from Sinoe
to Bassa, from the coast of Bassa to Monrovia,
from Monrovia to Robertsport.

The ocean begins its soft whistling, like a new widow
that first morning after her loss.
All the dead at the ocean's bottom, whose bones
still search for refuge.
From the Atlantic's bed, a song rises in the ocean currents.
It is their sound that comes and goes, at dawn,
when the night is splintered into invisible bits.

Pittsburgh

PATRICIA JABBEH WESLEY

This city of hills and rivers and steel,
always, the slant in the road,
the winding, falling cliffs, bridges, the escape
route, through which I come to find myself.
The city where, if you can cry loud
and hard, all you'll do
is replace river.
So, when the land comes sliding down
with house, pot, and pan during the rains,
you may not need to swim.
Your tunnels never lead me to the other place
I have lost, and in seeking to find
that place, I spill poetry
in small bits of broken crumbs,
in between the burnt metal pieces
of the past of my own city.
When I was a child,
I used to hear of this faraway place
where my people came to drown
themselves in search of America.
Pittsburgh, I do not know
if they found America, or if like me,
they came and went
away still longing for home.
Sometimes, for me, your roadways
lead to the Strip District for cassava roots
and fish and *gari* and sweet potato greens,
or sometimes, I find all the condiments

we could not bring with us
when we fled Africa.
So, I come to the Strip, where streets
are so jammed, if you do not pinch
yourself hard enough,
you might forget
you are not in an African market.

Pittsburgh, maybe someday
I may discover why you do not go away
even when I drive away to the small
town where I have buried myself
like a seed all these years.
Whether it is your merging rivers
or your hills rising into other hills
or your tunnels, or the ghosts
of my people who once lived here,
or just the wandering in my feet
looking for home,
I do not know.

Monrovia Women

PATRICIA JABBEH WESLEY

Monrovia women . . .
Here they come!
You see their colorful faces
before you know their hearts.
Shining, red lips, red cheeks,
painted eyelids and lashes.
Perhaps they would like
to paint their pupils too!
Their eyebrows take to various routes
to suit their longing hearts.

Aye, Monrovia women . . .
Look at their necks!
You could build a mansion
from jewelry a single woman wears.
Sometimes, like Indians,
their noses wear gold rings,
while their ears themselves
wear several others too.

You have yet to see their hands . . .
Long nails painted
to match the various hues
their eyes and cheeks wear.
Fingers held apart
by heavy gold rings.
Oh, you should see them
walking down the road.

Monrovia women . . .
In evening gowns and dresses,
lappa suits and costly coats,
on their way to work.
You should see them at work!
They nurse and paint their nails all day,
and guide their skirts from hooking
on to a rusty nail.

Monrovia women . . .
Strolling in the humid sun
in high, expensive shoes.
If you would stop
to ask their toes
how much fun it really is,
walking in such heels,
I'm sure you'd say *aye-yah*,
for our poor Monrovia women.

I'm Waiting

PATRICIA JABBEH WESLEY

I'm waiting for my grandchildren to come.
Waiting to rub down their little feet
with my tired hands, to hold them close
to my chest the way *Iyeeh* held me
when the birthing mothers lay me
in her brave arms in Dolokeh
where I was born, the *Toebo* child, born
in stranger land, *Chee Dawanyeno*,
stranger woman,
                they named me.

Waiting, so politicians can get that wake-up
moment, grow hearts inside, and be men.
Waiting for those babies in cages
across America's troubled heart to be freed.
Waiting for the immigration breakdown
of fences and hard people
with their barbed-wire hearts, snatching
hungry children from
                their mothers' arms.

Waiting for dawn, for the yellowing
of sun and the passing of moon.
Waiting for a kinder day to dawn.
I'm waiting so my neighbor's trees
can shed their leaves
                willingly.

Waiting for the snow, for the cold frosting
of ground and tree limbs, for cliffs
around this town where I have buried years
of my life, to lower themselves so the winds
can breathe for once, so new blood
can move upon this old town
and melt the cold in the shut-down hearts
of this town, oh, Altoona, how long
shall I be here to feel
              like belonging?

I'm waiting to someday see my mother
in Heaven, to hold her hand, to laugh and cry
and listen to her one more time.
Waiting to tell her how much I've discovered
in the places where she pointed me,
and how hard those places have become.
To kneel before her in search of forgiveness,
to do all the things I couldn't do before
she departed without
              bidding me farewell.

I'm waiting for women to take hold
of this broken world with their tenderness
of heart without which there would
be no earth, a world, ruined in unrepairable
places by people who have kept
              a blindness as their hope.

Yes, I'm waiting so women can walk
again, the way we were meant to walk
hard, on surfaces where men
have refused to walk. Waiting,
so, we can finally mend the pain of our broken

homelands, all the ruined places
of our being, oh Africa,
to mend our broken roads and broken minds.
I'm waiting so we can heal this world
                        for my grandchildren.

Waiting to turn my world over to my children,
before I someday pass on to the other world,
where our ancestral mothers have found
their own stools from which to reign, where
my own mother, Hne Dahtedor, sits,
                        waiting my arrival.

PART IV

Emerging and Aspiring Liberian Poets

Harper Nedee?

BARTH AKPAH

Where are the stamps
of feet of schoolboys
playing football
at Harper City Demonstration
playground, the hundreds of eyes
standing and cheering teams,
or mocking them for or against
victory?

Harper Nedee?
Who planted this Silence
in our streets and stole our tongues
at view centers when Chelsea plays
host to Barca at Stamford Bridge?

Harper Nedee?
Is there no moonlight dance
again, in our land, no leopard dance
to chase this savage fellow away
from our land?

Harper Nedee?
How did hand washing become a dance,
a ritual for cleansing at our doorsteps?
The new song is "united, we fall,
divided, we stand," our medicine men
calls it social distance—the Alleluia chorus
of Easter.

Harper Nedee?
Did you see billions of hearts, sanitized
in search of life, in search of death
in search of which party sings
the victory song—heaven or hell
when the pot is broken
and our eyes closed to death call?

Nedee?
Is it true that stalk by stalk,
our laughter is harvested
and fed to the groundhogs
and nematodes, by an invisible
—assailant—
whose songs we hate to hear,
whose songs we hear to hate.

Oche Dike Ala (Grandma Has Gone)

BARTH AKPAH

(Inspired by Patricia Jabbeh Wesley's Young Scholars of Liberia Workshop)

The Chair sits alone like a throne without
a king

like the river whose only source is barricaded and
sand-filled

when its lyrics trickle down the melody of
the earth.

The Chair sits alone with no one to tender its
rough handles

now, that Chair rings the alarm of life
as a slapstick

that life and its dreams are a pie
in the sky.

Today gave birth to a story whose villain
is grief,

and the protagonist is
Oche Dike!

Dike Ala! The iroko tree
has fallen!

Oche Dike, my song, she who gave breath
to my mother,

the mother who gave birth to me
and my song,

when the moonlight rang its bell for
her dance.

On whose tongues shall I run the errands
of words

when proverbs fell on the fringe
of my ears?

The Chair, yes that Chair, the occupant used
to sit

there in the heart of our hut to adjudicate
matters

of the heart as the chief head of Umu ada,
but here comes

to us, the comedy of life—death which
intrudes like

an untamed elephant from the zoo
rampaging

the neighborhoods with fear hanging on
its trunk,

and feet stamping the land in brazen-faced
eyes of death

whose songs, a dance for all mortals when one's
clogs are popped at the hour.

A Woman

JEE-WON MAWEIN ESIKA ARKOI

A woman's heart is round,
so, when it falls for you,
it rolls to the shape of you.
If you are smooth, it slips and slides.
If you're rocky, it goes up and down,
bouncing, rocking, dropping, shaking
and maybe, in the end, it breaks too.
If you're flat, it moves front, it moves back,
then it comes to a standstill.

A woman's heart is held to her chest
beneath her breasts,
and while it may seem hard to reach,
a woman's heart is forgiving.
If a woman should collect
the debt which she is owed,
even the sun would not rise or set.
For it would know no east or west,
and Men would know no day or night.

If a woman should collect the debt she is owed,
we would slaughter all the animals, drain their blood
and there still would not be enough to pay
for all the months she's cut
from the inside folded, and bled.

If a woman should collect the debt she is owed,
even the Oceans would run dry

trying to return all her water it broke,
so that men may come forth.
Generation after generation, her water spills
and without remorse, they celebrate
that her breaking means their birthing.

If a woman should collect the debt, she is owed
history would be impaired,
my country would have no civil war to blame,
for her flaws. You see, a woman birthed an Alhaji,
a Doe, a Taylor, a Quiwonkpa, a Yormie Johnson,
a Black Diamond, a Power, a Butt Naked.

If a woman should collect the debt she is owed,
the story of Liberia would remain untold.
There would be no Bowier, no Saye-Guannu, no Johnson-Sirleaf,
no Sankawolo, no Bai T. Moore, no Patricia Jabbeh Wesley,
no Kenneth Best, no Lekpele, no Wayetu, no WamaToh,
no Forte, no Me, no you.

If a woman should collect the debt she is owed,
all of humanity will become extinct,
trying to refill her body
with all the bodies she has pushed into this world.
You see, a woman is the belly she carries,
life, water, blood, bones, wars, stories, history, fire!

She is fire, so if she should collect,
the world would burn to ashes, and it would rain!
But a woman's heart is for giving,
Her heart loves this world so much
it would break and rain on only ashes.

If

JEE-WON MAWEIN ESIKA ARKOI

If I were a fly
I would want to fly
but I wouldn't want
to be a fly

If I were a fly
I would want
to be a bird
and if I were a bird

I wouldn't want
to be any bird
I would want
to be an eagle

If I became an eagle
I would want
to become the wind
But if I became the wind

I would want to be seen
So, I would then want
to be the sky
Now if I were the sky

I would want to feel
the ground
swim in the waters
eat the plants

play with the animals
hug somebody
be touched by somebody
have a human body

I would want to be human
even if I were
all of these things
I would still want
to be human for
it is human to want.

My Mother's Tale

JEE-WON MAWEIN ESIKA ARKOI

For my mother

She stood there on a Saturday morning,
painting a mental picture in her mind,
                watching the heavy downpour
that had begun the day before
but still didn't seem to be near the end.

Our bag of rice is empty, and if you know,
you know that you shouldn't play
with Liberian people's rice business.
In this Liberian household,
we eat country rice only.
She imagines the hassle she'll go through
to "find car." On this rainy, cold,
wet Saturday morning, she thinks
of the bean sauce she cooked on Thursday,
the one Baby Arkoi likes, but didn't enjoy
because she likes it with country rice,
not the imported *nyanmanyama*.

She imagines Gorbachev market, Red-Light,
where the *zogoes* hustle rain or shine,
where there is mud, red, thick, stinking mud.
She imagines the *portor, portor*,
but like a hen who has waited for the rain
that refuses to cease, like a hen,
that keeps her children warm
under her wings while her heart breaks
from watching them starve,

like a hen, that goes into the rain ignoring
the cold, searching for the last rice grain,
Mama Arkoi put on her boots, got herself ready,
and ran through our flooded yard, into the rain.
Looking for rice for us, her chicks,
                    my wonderful mother.
It's Sunday morning, and it's raining still,
Rev. Arkoi looks out the window,
pointing at the chickens in the rain.

Our *Desse*, my *Esika*, though from another world,
relates to that country chicken
more than *Mawein*, the Lorma people's stranger,
more than *Sumowuo*, a son of the soil.
Mama Arkoi looks at the chickens, and smiles
and then laughs, her laughter so alive
and sweet, like the melodies of her people,

like the Lingala songs from her people,
the Congolese people, who know how to sing
so well, songs I don't understand, but try to sing.
She laughs, thinking about yesterday's
trip to Red-Light Market.
Looking out the window, she says, "I remember."

While Tomorrow Waits

WATCHEN JOHNSON BABALOLA

We backbite, backstab, and backtrack
while tomorrow waits.
With pent up breath
in labor for far too long,
beads of anguish roll down her face,
yet she holds on hopefully
to the ebbing strength
needed to push into existence the precious cargo.
She carries a new dawn
of dreams and hope.

We trade in subterfuge of all shapes and hues,
while tomorrow waits
to hear the first faint cries of her young,
watch him grow stronger as he gulps
life-giving air into his fragile lungs,
fresh ideas and thoughts
To suckle at her breasts.
Drawing everything needed
to perfect the dream.
Not rundown or squalid,
but real, tangible, solid.

We tell lies, burglarize, and criticize
while tomorrow waits.
To train her wayward prince
persuaded to a life of *big boy-ism*,
a mirage-feeding, self-seeking, bottomless greed.
Fashioned by all that is unpatriotic.
She waits for that moment,
the lifting of the eyes
the clearing of the haze
the tearing of the veil
the peeling of the scales.

We agitate and desecrate.
We run late . . .
while tomorrow waits.

Divided We Stand

WATCHEN JOHNSON BABALOLA

Did the founding mothers
in their minds
envisage a nation torn
that day, when on our
lush, green height,
freedom raised her glowing form?

After surviving a "night of doom,"
did those women
dream for a moment
that liberty's star,
the promise of dawn,
would someday need atonement?

Did *Dawoe* dimly anticipate
the dishonor
of anointed ones?
Could *Nanporlor* predict
the defilement of choice?
The adornment of ills and wrongs?

But . . . here we are;
divided we stand
over wars and rumors of wars.
While the founding mothers
from their divine abode
stare, appalled at evil, galore.

New Kru Town, Where I Come From

EDWIN OLU BESTMAN

this is a township /
where kids await the raindrops
for shower /
their bodies painting pictures of
sorrow

teenage girls are mothers /
drug abuse and gangsterism is
street language /
surrounding, scattered like an
abandoned dumpsite

this is my home /
where violence is not a strange
soldier /
waking up to the sound of palava
& drumbeats

teenage boys are fathers /
where parents and children marry
the nightclubs /
where bread winners fall victim to
married & unmarried people

this is my home /
where the streets sleep naked /
rape & sodomization are known
celebrities

water floods our homes /
corruption is a beautiful first
class citizen /
dreams are aborted babies

the air isn't safe /
we're afraid of inhaling &
exhaling /
drinking water is another idiot
damaging our stomachs

Okada boys are hustlers too /
ridding unsafely through
communities /
maybe we lost our love to our descendants

Darkness, the Surname of a Poor Lover

EDWIN OLU BESTMAN

I

I met this pretty girl / she had transparent lips with no color / castled
my proposal in her bones

II

Every 60 seconds makes a minute / but a clock never ripped her eyes /
our love became a lonely cemetery

III

I mourned the broken things / exchanged dreams with nightmares /
my body fell naked

IV

How I wished to possess her skin / washed away bloody tears / but
her eyes made romance to a rich man's pocket

V

She was black / photocopy of her complexion / her desires rise like
the tides of the ocean

VI

My love lay wrapped in a piece of cloth / kisses like the nights / I lost
my bride to a stranger

How to Write a Dirge for Liberia

EDWIN OLU BESTMAN

Begin with its North, that is covered in crystal tears,
lips that dip, dwell, and drown into silence,
with a heart that sleeps in a scattered field.

Find a route to the West,
the West that births darkness amidst the day.
Sweeps the smile that lights our way,
and writes stories on bitter leaves.

Get down to the East,
where we live beneath the grass,
where our stomachs sing songs of sorrow,
and poverty is our next-door neighbor.

Sink down to the South,
where the streets are wrapped with bits of rubbish,
where the homeless are broken and stuck
between rusty iron bars.

Let's begin with the government.
Tell how it employs cockroaches and rats
to stir the affairs of her reserve.
They are the thieves brandishing their pockets
with the fruits of her womb.

End with either an exclamation mark!
Throw your sadness away,
and roll up your sleeve for another life.

Memories of Home

EDWARD K. BOATENG

No one leaves home unless home is the mouth of a shark.
—WARSHAN SHIRE

In a land where the chicken's crow is substituted with guns
We find it easy to carry our load / through unknown routes
with hopes of quenching our thirst in another man's land. For
our walls have wounds and scars
But we fear the reception / that they will say

"we smell of corpses" or "our eyes hold the images of bloodshed"
& "our skins are fossils of the very war they fear"
I want to peel off these scars 1990 left us / &
rename them after the bodies of my siblings
But peeling them hurts as much as leaving them. And
talking about them just reminds me of the same war songs

they sang over the city they turned into a cemetery

Curing My Mother's Wound

EDWARD K. BOATENG

We looked for peace, but no good came; for a time of healing, but behold, terror.
            —JEREMIAH 8:15

So, we keep feeding this old sore
with the same salt
that dug the marrow from our bones
Sometimes . . .
we get tired of driving away "pupu flies"
that keep humming old war jingles over this broken skin.
For this one wound has caused us to bury unsung songs
in the hollow of our throats
Since 1990 . . .
Mama lay before this pool
awaiting the Savior to command her, "Take up your mat and walk."
But our saviors have lost their powers to heal
while picking pockets in a land, where all the coins were melted to
    bullets

Genealogy of the Fourteen Pieces of Liberia

EDWARD K. BOATENG

Slavery begat negro / & negro begat Liberia / & Liberia begat war / &
   war begat death
. . . this death
birthed us in depression / unmended bodies,
hosting broken souls
In 1990, we drowned the sun in Mama's bucket & lit darkness in the
   roof of our house
Now . . . our eyes are weary from carrying the heaviness of the dark
. . . and this darkness
lit the road to our house of sorrows / gathered our mother's sweat and
   buried it
in the belly of the earth
So, all our lips sing / "sorrow after sorrow / after sorrow / after
   sorrow!"

Maybe I'll Go Home

EDWARD K. BOATENG

For (Ade) Patricia Jabbeh Wesley

The words sit in my mouth,
"Maybe I'll go home."
I want to use my tongue
like a spoon, to dish them out.

Sssh! Mommy cuts me off.
Home reminds her of the smell of death
& the memories our cities wear
or maybe, she's afraid that I'll become
another *zoko* who lives with the streets,
like another child soldier / without war,
just fighting angry ghosts left by the war.

She tells me, "This country is green
and gives us many opportunities to live."
Reasons we have to live / like prisoners of war
in another man's land,
buying hatred with our color.

A fate that even our characters didn't change.
My name labors from their mouth like a forceful vomit,
& when they see me, they say, "What refugee has the audacity
to soar over us with skin as dark as her home,
harvesting our sun to hang in their darkened skies?"

He Stole a Piece of Me

TETEE ALEXANDRA BONAR

He stole a piece of me.
It was the day after Saturday,
after the songs of the morning birds,
between the smiles and frowns of the day.
I got stoned and went out of guard
Sunday, at 6 o'clock.
Half dead, half alive
stiff, barely breathing, eyes blinking, ears locked,
I lay at the equator of death and life.
Four eyes, two teary, two desperate.
Two set of lips, one, pleading, the other, demanding.
School or home teacher came to rape
his student, instead of teaching.
His venom, the poison.
I'm not normal.

Gosh, I'm swollen!
Fragile story, broken virginity
my school or home teacher
actually raped me?
Unbelievable.

One year, two years, Seven years!
The slaps and punches, and oh,
the bruises are gone, his lies, his threats,
my evidence have all disappeared.
But a piece of me was stolen!

Identity

CHORLYN E. CHOR

Those straight paths lead to our town, and that's our farm.
There, we build huts, scratch farms,
and drink wine from palm trees.

There, we tell stories of great heroes and legends.
There, talents are spilled around firewood.
You see those stones forming a circle.
There, I remember how Grandpa
told us tales of warriors, their bravery and their patriotism,
and sometimes, Grandma joined those telling
us that girls ought to learn cooking, cleaning
caretaking, and to be housewives.
That other route,
it leads to the city—Monrovia—
we once called city of Christ, but now it's
just James Monroe's namesake.
That same route also leads to liberty and peace,
according to Grandpa.
He would say, "Hold on, look from where
we are standing, to the Wutevi, and down to Lake Piso
and to the Cavalla; look at the capes
and islands and then the peninsulas."

Grandpa would say that's what we gained—
That's not all, he would say, "We gained liberty
and independence; we gained a place
from which we cannot
be deported."

That's what we gained when our ancestors
were brutally beaten and hanged
to die for reasons yet unknown,
Grandpa would say, "The clay beneath our soles,
they aren't Black,
they are blood,
blood of our ancestors, waging wars for freedom
and peace."
And beneath the clay, they left us fertilizers
and humus.
From the blood and bodies buried beneath our feet
to show where they lay in the glory of their defeat.
For death wasn't a punishment,
death was liberation.
Our ancestors fought the fight
and drowned in their sweat.
So, we could use them as floaters to save the land.

You Are Mine

SUNNY EDDIE CRAWFORD

From the day of our independence
in 1847
my heart's been longing for you like the flowing cavalla.

At the twinkle of the light,
which rises from the south of Monrovia,
my heart thirsts for you.
You're like the beauty of the Sapo National Park.
How I long for more of the sweetness
that rises beyond the surface of Mount Wologizi.

Oh! Beauty of the Lorma tribe,
you are my oxygen.
That air my lungs inhale and exhale
on the bed rocks of Cape Mount
where your love smokes my heart like a dry fish,
our mothers prepared for evening dinner.

Come let's build the palace of love
in my veins
in the veins of the body of a Grebo boy.
We'll sign a promise on the hills of Ducor
where the breeze from the Atlantic clamps my soul
to press the vow of agreement
that "You are mine."

Words in Portrait

SUNNY EDDIE CRAWFORD

I clashed with my skiff memory,
one wrestling sunny day
under a tropical shade.
The waving plum trees,
silent settlement,
of many Liberian imaginations.
Most likely a narrow place,
for me to rest my thoughts,
create impressive thoughts,
out of thoughts,
restructuring them.
Of a girl who dotted down,
dugout of fear,
caged my dying heart in ecstasy.
Sketch out her undiluted beauty,
printed her unfaded golden portrait,
in a silver blossom color wax,
a wooden frame of beautiful art.
My wind-searching eyes,
raced after her in Monrovia.
Her big round blue eyes,
beautiful as the blue lake,
in Tubmanburg,
magnifies the Liberian setting.
Hair, curly, soft, and black,
like a day-old banana leaf.
Her melanin-charcoal skin,
smooth as the coastal beaches in Kakata.
A tender feature,
of an African orchid.

Deepu

A Definition of Divinity   ARTHUR SHEDRICK DAVIES

For a mother so loves her children
that she gives her very self,
that they, if ever should believe in her,
shall not perish but inherit perpetual paradise.

Somewhere on the Grain Coast,
the tenderness of affection in a mother's name—Deepu—
sinks deeper than the "pu" (as in pool) it purifies.

My leaping bones have tasted the glory
lustering in her love as the gleam glitters
to worlds afar, surpassing measurable degrees.

She embodies motherhood beyond the ordinary:
Brushing through bushes and feeding flames, simultaneously,
to the belle of a hungry fire hearth—leading a dual role,
as the wo and man of our healthy hut.

It's no secret that her body is unleavened bread.
I've noticed how she bruises and breaks herself daily,
furnishing homes and mopping floors
with the stings of her flesh.

That her children "might have life,
and have it more abundantly." She reminds me
of the Lord's Supper.

Redemption is no easy endeavor,
knowing that a piece of you must die each day
before the final death. I guess this is what the Messiah meant
when He murmured:

"Greater love hath
no man [woman]
than this . . ."

That a mother
lays down her life
for her pekins.

Her blood must be the fruit of the vine: upon every sundown,
she sprinkles a handsome portion on our doorposts,
soaking them with heavier chants of "Amens,"
as she demands the demons of death

to pass us over—a vesper of power,
to which the little devils must flee with fright
at its utterance!

Dear Oldma,

Blessed are thou among oldmas.

These are testaments
that the Father
has bestowed you
with

a name above all other names.

And here, I'll always stand—confident.
With my heart, strong, and gaze locked on a tick-tocking clock,
awaiting the last days when the rapture erupts,
that I may root my shadow beneath the skin of your wings
as we transcend above angels.

With immortal seeds, sowed in the lips of our cells,
sprouting out as heavenly gems, to be harvested
in a realm where souls never die!

Somewhere on the Grain Coast, Deepu always will be
the name of the Daughter of Man—Mama—endowed with such
    similar love
which brought salvation down to earth, the love which spells out

the definition of a divine miracle!

Origins of the Poet Next Door

ARTHUR SHEDRICK DAVIES

For the voices,
afraid of being heard

before
the beckoning dawn,
you were forged from
stardust, as anthologies,

to store
the mysteries of
a million seas; drawn from
river sprouts, bearing multitudes

of reincarnations,
in your body cells, to immortalize
daylight, to dismiss the dark, and
reconstruct fertility in the bellies of
barren dreams; from oasis your blood

was composed,
to quench the thirst from
the desert's throat, to spring
the forest, and the dead lands,
back to life. your root is rooted beyond

the stars;
you were pottered from
the breath of a superior God,
to rewrite the sun and the moon; to melt
chaos, to drown perplexity, and bury grief
with pieces of poems, poured on a page.

This Is Poetry

ARTHUR SHEDRICK DAVIES

This is poetry:
An affectionate conveyance of language,
the reconciliation of feelings and emotions
channeled through the creative lenses of imagination.

A world, endowed with endless possibilities,
its galaxy, a beautiful mixture of metaphors,
mending wounds molded by mountains.

Like the profound prayer in the Psalms,
it is a green pasture in paradise
where passion encounters the presence of peace—

And peace becomes a realm of healing
to a field of shattered souls
who thirst for a sip of hope in written words.

This is poetry,
a safe haven to outcasts that were torn
by multiple blades, the land where
Elijah never dies, Goliath remains slain,
and Lazarus always resurrects.

Free Me

MAUREEN JENNIFER DAVIES

Free me from your endless rumors.
I speak the way I do
because I was taught in school
that my subject and verb should agree.
            And that's a rule.
I'm sorry if you didn't pay much attention
in school, but don't dare tell me
I'm trying to speak *seerees*
            or that I sound American.
I don't always have to speak colloquial
to prove I'm from LIB,
so, free me!

Free me from your bizarre stereotypes.
Don't question me being a Lorma girl
because I don't have a big backside.
I know that you think that my "behind"
            is flatter than a door.
You think you're rubbing it in,
but you cannot because
I like being me.
Free me!

Free me from your ruthless gossip.
Don't go explaining that I'm too young
            to be a mother.
I was naive and lost, always in the wrong
places, with the wrong people,

but that's not your business.
You saw me . . . all the time
when I needed a hand to lead me.
You did not make it your business
to give advice.
Now, make it not your business
to gossip about my child and me.

Free me from your labels.
Yes, you say I'm a talkative,
but I have a right to contribute
to conversations.
So, don't dare tell me I like to *fuller-place*.
Free me!
Free me!
I like my "sentimentality"
I like my slimness; I like my laugh,
the way I talk, and I like
the way I makeup my face.
I just love being me, and I'm never
going to fit the space
you've carved up for me.
So, free me!

Our Mother Is Gold

ESSAH COZETT DIAZ

She is salt and sand,
shady from seeds that never grew.
She is not God, not perfect,
not your friend.

Sometimes she is loud
and controlling like the wind.
You cannot tell her no;
she will swallow you up
in a prayer because the Lord says
"vengeance is mine!"

She never knew the answers,
but she tarried all night,
fasted all day, to make sure
your path was somewhat straight.

She is not God, can't create
life on her own. Don't you
know that you are the rainbow
that appeared six times.

Seven is the number of completions.

She is not whole.
She is woman,
flaws and salt.

She is water.
Sometimes shaky, other times
solid as a rock.
She is all matter, energy,
spirit, flesh.

She is not God; she is your mother.

When a Rolling Stone Leaves Pebbles Behind

ESSAH COZETT DIAZ

For my birth father

I know the meaning of my name is *Thank You*,
my patronymic has changed because of you.

My Oma says your *papay* had an "open gate" smile,
walkabout the village causing *wahala* like you.

At Grandpa's funeral, my cousins told me about the wedding
saying that my surname comes from you.

The whispers that come through the winds
at night remind me that spirits do linger, *dah* you?

Not too sure if this is a dream or a nightmare I am living,
but reality is full of betrayal, something, I learned from you.

¡Cuando escucho la palabra *Negra* pienso en *Libertad*
pero los coquíes no cantan igual si no hay hembras, *y tú?*

How many ways can you spell absence?
The first letter must always start with you.

I cannot stare at the moon too long or think of raising a child.
Big belly woman smells like copper pennies and breastmilk to you.

Your name was vacuumed from my lips,
my menstrual cycle only lasts three days 'cause of you.

The next generation will believe they are the first

living in the silence that replaced my last name, oh you.

Thank God I come from a tribe of praying Vai women
who name their children hallelujahs and Essahs, unlike you.

For Daughters Who May Never Be Mothers

ESSAH COZETT DIAZ

I

All we have in common is distance;
and death, because of   distance.

II

Had sea not swallowed my mother's seeds,
    I would have learned to breathe under water.

Her fears became mine,
    and I learned how to swim.

Arms up swinging,
    until treading water became breath.

Black pepper flowers bud in Georgia red clay.
    Surviving should come naturally,

but my unborn siblings did not want that responsibility.

III

Blue and black cohosh
bathe in a calabash; sip
my bloodstream relief.

Tribal-mark tattoos
sharp like a silk-cotton tree
remind me of her.

IV

Así de frágil el tiempo es.
Firstborns become burdens
become mold for the rest.
How sure are we that life is certain?

There is time to change tradition.
Nuevas flores florecen todos los días
rebelling earthly conditions.
Do they see us?

A vulcano errupts at sea
no one is there to protest.
Somos como el moriviví,
maybe we are more than blessed.

For Women Who Are Water in Fields of Rice

ESSAH COZETT DIAZ

Defeat comes in the dawn of mourning as silence slips off lips of a midwife. / She wipes a mother's blood against her ivory print *lappa*—their fingers paint misery. / Before her first was born, six *sahsahs* rattled, yet no one cries to carry spirit. / Maybe if she would stop chewing off her fingernails, blood would have a chance to dry. / Women in her family only know love through sacrifice. / They raise children that other mothers produce—sharing milk of their stillborn to save the futures of a fading village. / When she washes, she scoops shadows from her skin. / No one mentions that her insides smell like Callery pear trees. / No praise songs here. / There are hums in winds that carry wanderers to far away cities. / Tonight, she drags offerings towards Lake Piso, mixing palm oil between remnants of her openings. / Each cavity transports phantoms that do not transition well. / Maybe next lifetime, she will return as a man, so when her children eject out of her openings, she does not bleed for centuries. /

From Coal Pots to Gas Stoves

ESSAH COZETT DIAZ

What if I told you, *I get it now.*

Bottles of palm oil sit on the kitchen counter—almost empty.
Red stained dishes pile up in the sordid sink.
Onions are the aroma on my flesh.

I am layered with languages and lands
foreign to me, yet the only nation I know
is my body, sí.

When the stew begins to boil,
I uncover the pot, releasing
what's left of our culture.

Maybe it was yours first,
but I can claim it now.
I am a garden of cassava leaves and pawpaw trees,

reaching towards heaven, or
wherever my ancestors meet.
I can't recall the last time I opened a recipe book.

I just close my eyes and let ingredients speak.
There is still loneliness in your voice;
you sound like Grandma.

Her lines appear on your face,
and I wonder if I will wear the same mask one day.

What if I told you, *I have found you*?

Under my stained pots, a pile of salt
anchors my anointing.
Sometimes, things we want to forget,

return in different forms.
I pray my child does not know your pain,
does not wrestle with tongues and intangible things.

I pray when they enter la cocina,
grounding meets their feet,
balance is in
the making,
        the molding,
                the shift.

So here I sit, unearthed.
The mainland and motherland
are reflected on this island.

At least this burning fire
will cleanse the path for the coming.
What if I told you, *I understand*?

I Wasn't Ready to Open My Eyes

For Habibullah Heban

Your words crawled through my ears
writing new lyrics on my eyelids.
Sometimes while we sleep,
God speaks to us in dreams.

You were gentle with me,
like a Shepherd to his sheep.
Sometimes life is easier when you
think sleeping and death are kin.

Last night, you came back to me.
No darkness ever surrounded you—
a bioluminescent bay of beginnings.
Maybe back then, we could've built a home.

Take the wood from my forest,
prepare and quiet place to pray.
It has been eight years since
I heard your dulcet voice.

They say you will never open
your eyes again. You will
no longer be my Somali Oud player.

Who will sing me a Balwo tonight?

The Brown Beauty

MAWATA DUKULY

The brown beauty, a natural color
that sparkles and shines brighter
than the sun.
The brown beauty,
a color full of cuteness.

The brown beauty,
have you seen how gorgeous her brown beauty is?
How blue and sparkling her eyes are?
Her hair is long, black and matches the brown beauty.
Her brown beauty is attractive and glowing.

The brown beauty
Her nose is short and matches the beauty of her face.
Her mouth, very tiny and pretty.
Her lips are a natural pink from God,
and her face and skin are spotless.

The brown beauty
Her eyebrows are pretty
and her chin.
If you are blessed with brown beauty,
then why bleach your skin?
The color brown is attractive
and her skin shines
bright like the sun.

Who Is a Leader?

MAWATA DUKULY

A leader—who is he?
A caretaker or
care seeker?
A truth teller or
teller of lies.
A lone sofa rider
Or merrymaker?

He is a good leader
For he comforts, tells truth, empathizes and shares with the have-nots

And ...

A bad leader inflicts pain and swims in lies.
His heart is a cloudy sky.

He is, but the served and killjoy—the modern Pharaoh

The Oppressed

JAMES VARNEY DWALU

Go ahead; laugh!
Laugh at me
with your mandibles, shaking
like a crooked zinc house
in the strong wind.
Laugh at your powerless slave
who yields to his master's whip.
If these strong arms of mine
could only . . .
O, let me not speak so
God is my avenger

I Am Nothing (Neutrality)

JAMES VARNEY DWALU

I am the cold light peering from afar
watching you sleep the night away.
The rivers, flowing smooth.
The calm oceans, sailing ships
and feeding men.
The bee that makes honey.

I am the hot light
burning your backs as you labor
the angry, rushing rivers
breaking your bridges, flooding your homes
the rough oceans,
sinking ships
and drowning men.
I am the bee that stings.
I hate, I love, I live.
To me, I am nothing!

Where Were You?

CYNTHIA SENU GAILOR

So, we have once more come together.
This time it is for the last time.
You have come to see me,
but there is a problem.
I cannot see you.

You have come to speak words
about our relationship, what I meant to you,
but I cannot hear you.
You have come to pay respect to me,
but I cannot appreciate it now.
Where were you?
When I needed someone to talk to,
you were not there.
When I was struggling to make ends meet.
Some days, my meal was only bread
and mayonnaise.
Some days, I neither had the money
nor the means to move around,
so, I walked this city mile upon mile.

Many days I had malaria,
I had severe fever, sometimes I was sick
because of malnutrition.
Where were you?
Some days I had to use a candle
and not a flashlight
because that was all I could afford.

Some days, I wish I had a better bed to lie on,
a better room to live in, and wished
I had nicer clothes to wear,
Where were you?
I know often times
you wanted to help me,
but you had to take care of yourself
and your own family first.
I know you had the heart,
but you didn't have the hand.

Where were you when I needed
someone to talk to, to share my dreams,
my goals, my aspirations, and my hopes?
Yes, I know you wanted to visit me
but you were too busy to stop by;
you had more important things to do.
Today I am dead and gone,
and cannot hear the beautiful words.
I cannot smell and taste the tasty meals
that you are now preparing
to consume over my body.
I will not be able to smile with you.
Where were you?

Don't beat yourself up,
I did not come to stay forever.
You may not have done your best
for me, but you can go and help somebody else.
Life is too short to hold grudges
and to procrastinate those

lofty ideals we want to carry out.
I am in the brother,
and I am in the sister
that is sitting next to you.
When you help them, you have helped me.
I am your friend—Jesus.
In as much as you have done
it to the least of these,
you have done it unto me.

Quarantine in Hope

DANIEL W. GARTEH JR.

Today, the Nimba mountain feeds tears to the St. John River,
and silence weds the waves of the Atlantic Ocean.

State of emergency has taken our streets by storm,
as isolation kidnaps the Lone Star.
Social distancing is now our new religion.

Nothingness takes front seat in classrooms,
hopelessness, the only food for the poverty-stricken.
Marketers walk the thin line of poverty.

Hospital beds hug the infected, but the spirit of recovery
holds isolation centers hostage, and survival is their ransom.

Health workers swallow their oaths before leaving their homes.
All they ask is that we stay at home.
They've sold their souls to faith.
Even the sand on the beaches is singing their praises.

Africa

CHERBO GEEPLAY

Africa, this sun
drenched bliss,
come to Botswana
and see the terrific
translucent creeks
of Okavango Delta,
   as it blends with
   the sun rays and
glistens. Let the
unmistaken eyes
catch the stretched
neck zebra, graceful
—game in the name
   of Africa. Its
   beautiful furs
decorated in broad
strokes, rising in
circular waves,
from head, to hind.
Now feast your eyes
on the herd of elephants
and the desert radiant
   landscape of the
   Savute—Africa,
oh Africa! The
motherland ever so
enchanting; the beautiful
safari, and her beautiful

subtropical wasteland,
home to the Kalahari.
  Then, see the
  overstretched
sandy, salient
desert, as she
greets the Tourag
of Mali. Supple
as their camels, nomads
and traders of the Sahara.
  Then the colossal
  evergreen forest,
wildlife, and the
plateaus of Liberia.
From palm to palm,
crystal clear beaches
along the Atlantic,
vista. Thrilling oasis
of waters from the
Congo to Lake
Victoria. The land
of my Fathers and
—its stunning rapture
  Africa, oh Africa.
  Then, let me glean
with naked eyes
the loveliness
of the Table Mountains
in Cape Town, and live
in Soweto for a day,
a borough of feisty warriors.
  To stomp my feet as
they do when they dance
and protest unreservedly.

In the land of the quiet
giant, who took on and
beat Robin Island
with glee, then
crushed it to
dust in one palm.
    Spectacular
    chronicle
for generations.
The land of the Pharos,
the beautiful—Africa oh, Africa!

The Diary of an Orphan

ALOYSIUS S. HARMON

I write this poem for the orphans.
Those that have dreamed to discern
the touches of parents,
and for others that are exhausted
of keeping prayer requests of depression
under their tongues.

This is for them,
that do not have homes to dream about the future,
for them that reserve pain in their bodies,
and for those that struggle to pick up
oxygen from dumpsites.

I write this poem, for those that have grief
reflecting smiles, for the sick, and the blind,
the ones, screaming from thunderstorms
under the cold.
To them whose skin suffered sunburns
from sleeping on market tables.

I write this poem, for rape victims,
for the underprivileged,
to those that see life as a nightmare.
For the broken and depressed
from years of starvation and poverty.

Pain as Metaphor

ALOYSIUS S. HARMON

Death is not for tightening your face
in a tight wooden coffin,
nor to dress in your favorite costume
　　to silently whisper goodbye.
It is an attire that is worn on the body
　　　　　　after birth.

Nothing burns more than the cold that sleeps
in our lungs, the shots
that cause our skin to wrinkle, and the hunger
that creates the void that you see
in our collar bones.

I remember the bullet songs of the wars,
in the 1990s, and how they penetrated
　　our skins with silent holes,
leaving bodies
entrapped under the red mud.

West Point, Liberia

ALOYSIUS S. HARMON

Welcome to my home that hosted
the burial of my umbilical,
                a home, beautified with zinc,
old doors, where drug abuse
is the fashion our brothers and sisters wear.

A place where abusive words snooze
under the tongues of teens,
                serve their bodies to men
for money, and boys paint their lungs
black from cigarettes smoke.

Take me on a tour of the township
                of West Point, where,
on Sundays, clubs sing praises to the gods
of poverty, where nakedness, is clothing
the youngsters wear.

Welcome to my home, West Point,
                a place where our bellies
hold emptiness and our skin makes
love with discomforts
only poverty can bestow.

Nah Fooh, Nah Fooh

RUBY M. HARMON

Nah fooh! Nah fooh!
Feet strike ground
dirt
hard in sync with syncopated melodies
rolling off the tongues.

The two girls with skirts drawn up
greet
and speak through feet
striking ground.

Entranced, the two,
and those around cheer,
yelling, "The girl's good, oh."

One throws the right leg,
lifting hips, weaving, then the left
hands echoing the dance.
Shoulders punctuate
heads bob, watching the feet of the other
as lips chant

nah fooh, nah fooh,
the crowd hmms and ohhs.

They are all waiting their turns
to pair up and compete.

The ground waits their knocking
feet . . .

Grey Stone Blues

RUBY M. HARMON

For Liberian war survivors

Kiss-meat . . . our lips had not forgotten
pursed around the black striations
the well of darkness
drawing in the miniscule, bittersweet meat
lodged in the river, strewn detritus
waste from war.
We lay our bodies twisted,
on flat rocks, sod, patches of green, grass,
we sought life.
We let raucous laughter spring from our hearts,
even when tomorrow seemed uncertain.
Aching for relief, our feet stepped
between bits of human
waste, as we sought water nearby.
Metal shots pierced the air.
We hid behind a fence, crept
as rockets riddled dilapidated buildings.
Breadfruit, mango trees wavered, their fruits
flung to the ground.
Those of us behind the fence felt
protected. Crowded and enclosed, we were
our own comfort. Morning brought
bright rays of sunshine, hope, but then the hunger.
Some may have lost their minds:
fragile, balanced, but we knew
deep inside, the spirit sought hope.
Did we want to endure, survive, overcome?
We tasted tiny bits of chance

sprinkled like salt, flavoring our dry rice and palm oil.
Wide-mouthed, our bellies licked its lips
relished the pleasure, anticipated the change.
What would night bring,
with its blue-grey presence;
its wide embrace, lending shelter?
Hands, clasped, we took deep breaths.
Willingly, our spirits embraced the morning.

Mother and Daughter

RUBY M. HARMON

My daughter, Musu, has forgotten
our custom
of respect.
See,
how she stands akimbo
talking to elders
expressing her new individuality.
Necessary in this new culture
rejecting traditional dress
for jeans, body-gloved
and blouses so low.
Her bosom peeks out.
Her ears stay glued to ear
phones, listening to lyrics
that degrade and belittle
her very own person.

And do you know what she tells me
when I mention her attitude?
She says, "How can you judge me when
you too have sought to be
different? Applying that lightening cream
to your beautiful black skin,
fading the person I once knew."
Imagine that.
My own Musu.

Imagine that . . .

We Need to Pass It On

QUITA HARVEY

The chair now sits alone.
Our culture and traditions are being abandoned,
and washed away with time.
Liberian youth are buried in western culture,
yet we claim
it's civilization.
We are in a modern age

with no ears for our own languages
Poro and Sande Societies are rainfall in the deserts.
Our norms and values, hidden away,
leaving us in complete darkness.
We are the vulnerable lost.

Where are those days,
when boys were initiated into manhood
and girls into womanhood
the days of unity
the days young and old gathered
to celebrate our culture?
Where are the days
when our fathers wrestled,
drummed, and chanted traditional songs
under the moonlight?

Where are the days
when our mothers danced to the drum,
pounded by our fathers

to the rhythms of their chanting?
Swaying their hips
and breaking their backs
while elders watched, nodding their heads,
and clapping their hands in amusement?

We need to break the barrier,
solve the puzzle,
return to our roots
and redeem our culture and traditions.
We need to teach our norms and values.
We need to keep our culture alive.
We need to pass it on. . . .

One World, One People

LAUREL ILOANI

Last night, in my dream,
black angels dancing, to and fro,
upon the downward stairs,
from the heavenly gate,
proclaiming a word the earth has never known.
I was blind and deaf
and could not see nor hear the angels.
Deep was I in earthly things

until I heard them say,
Jesus is the son, the Lord,
and also Mohammed is the son, the Lord.
I trembled at the sight.
My ears kept blocking my hearing,
and I pretended it was a joke.

I could hear them saying aloud,
Jesus is black, Jesus is white.
Whatsoever you take him to be,
he is, and I was baffled, my mind lost itself,
trying to believe,
what my world never believed.
With fear, I heard the words of the angels,
who beheld me, stronger than true love.
And I could not resist their words.

I could hear them saying again,
We're the angels of truth and purity,

fear not. For you're the chosen one.
Tell your world,
the truth, they never knew.

Oh, I replied, in a deep heavy voice,
I fear, they won't believe me.
And I will become a caricature.

My world kills the innocent for nothing.
Color, religion, luxury kills us.
In one voice aloud, they replied,
Go into the world,
and spread what you have heard.
For our God (Allah) is with you.
Tell them, they are;
One world, one people.

I bowed my head and cried.
With a pain filled voice, I said,
My world has been in darkness
for these centuries.

I could hear them say, in a powerful voice,
strong as the wind,
Go, go,
you have no time to spare.

The Ebola Ride

PATRICE JUAH

On the Ebola ride,
paranoia is the driver.
It takes you on a high
and leaves your senses
hanging in the wild.

Fear is its deputy,
and panic, the conductor.
You never know
which way the bus will go,
but you are told,
that as long as you stay put,

wash your hands
and limit human contact,
you're safe, at least for a while.
You do your best
to secure your seat,
making sure your loved ones
are safely on board.

But as death news comes in,
you're reminded,
this isn't a normal ride.
You get a sudden kick,
a silent voice asking,
why you're still here.
Perhaps on a mission,
or for a purpose?

Then suddenly, gratitude takes over,
as you give thanks
for still being alive.
And this is all happening
on the Ebola ride.

Still on the road, pickups rush by
with men dressed like aliens,
either carrying or going
to pick up fallen victims.

Somewhere in a Containment Unit,
a baby cries in horror,
as his mother takes her last breath.

You peek through the window,
crowded streets create the illusion
of a normal life; but as alive
as everything appears from the outside,
fear is killing us slowly on the inside.

Sometimes we wonder
who'll get off next,
but that's the Ebola ride:
No traffic lights, no horns,
no road signs,
just us against an unseen enemy.

The night brings relative calm,
but we rarely sleep,
as the nightmare of
what's to come the day ahead
haunts our dreams.

And on the other side,
the ocean wind sets the flames
in the Crematorium ablaze,
as our hearts leap
for the souls of the ones dearly loved—

No last goodbyes,
only memories, anguish,
pain and grief.
We're stuck on this bumpy ride,
with tiny doses of hope.
And though help arrives,
we're still in doubt,
as they too are clueless
about when the ride will end.

So, world, we're here,
on this handwashing,
temperature-taking,
Emotion-wrecking, friends-avoiding
hugs-and-handshakes-prohibiting,
nonstop Ebola ride.

An Afro-Madrileña Love Note

PATRICE JUAH

Madrid, my darling,
where have they taken you?
I see you stare in a distance,
voice caged, head bowed.
Desolate parks,
empty streets,
but yet so dainty.
I sigh. I gasp. I watch.
Your familiar allure
holds me spellbound
drawing me in.
Amidst the eerie silence,
I blink back to reality.
Your charm,
so ever-present
A mesmerizing dance of rainbows
beckons to fill
a void in a hallowed space.
Your glory lurks in the shadows,
soaring beyond despair.
Grief so profound
only time can erase.
Your cafes and hidden treasures sigh,
yearning for relief.
History, nestled beneath your cracks and walls
sweetheart, what unimaginable gloom has befallen you?
In awe and dismay,
I reflect,

of what was, what is, and what could come next.
Reminiscing:
The very first day I met you,
long walks exploring you,
lunches way past lunch hour,
and dinners turned midnight carefree chattering.
Like a forgotten memory,
the days fade away,
bursting free your spirit.
Rising like the Phoenix that you are,
cementing resilience with each balcony cheer.
Courage intact,
fear unmasked
just like you were when we first met.
My loyalty remains.
And right beside you I'll always stand—
Steady. Hopeful. Confident.
Of healing, laughter and adventures.
Of the smell of freshly brewed coffee and
tortillas straight from the heart
I've been in this abyss before.
A déjà vu on wings.
But trust me when I say, you shall rise.
Your willpower steers your path,
a forward march until the fight is won.
Though the melodies seem to wane
and the hugs long disappeared,
I hope the chirping birds deliver this love note to you.
a reminder that this Afro-Madrileña
continues to dream of you.

Ebony Perfection

MCCHEN A. D. KANNEO

She's dark like shell of a kernel.
In her world, lipsticks don't exist.
Her lips shine like they sleep in oil,
her hair, thick and curly.

It's like she ages with beauty,
her entire being, flawless,
even wrinkles are allergic to her face.
If I could cage a finger,
her finger will be a prisoner.
For she's a fountain of glitters
in a galaxy of perfection.

The Making of Grief

JEREMY TEDDY KARN

I

Out of cries I have made songs
I sometimes
    hum in my sleep deep under my skin

I dig memories out of my body,
plant silence in it.
    I have watched my silence grow into nothing
My mother says, it can move a mountain

II

There are things sadder than death,
    like smoke that gains its existence
from a body on fire

The way cigarettes burn in Monrovia
reminds me of you dead & burning in the brown soil

It stripped you into ashes,
    but a body on fire is the origin of grief
The fumes from your burnt body,
I have lived with the scent long enough.

Elegy for a Friend

JEREMY TEDDY KARN

Of course, you / held your phone out the window
& snapped photos of the wind [*for memories sake*]

You rolled up your skin / like a map / every time
you ran out of roads.

Months back, laughter fell off / your mouth
watching trees in / the rear mirrors follow / your car into the wind.

Maybe you were racing with the clouds . . .

Your heart on fire / to see the other side
of the country / where the blue sky ends in a small river

Maybe this is how every road trip ends . . .

The blue pavement so eager / to hold your blood in its mouth . . .
It has made a road map of your body.

My First Winter

EVELYN KEHLEAY-MILLER

I sat shaking, wide-eyed,
shaking not from the cold, but from the place.
It looked bare and burned to me,
and I thought the leaves would never be restored.

This I did from day to day,
weeping softly for the beloved greenery.
I cursed the gods for this negative karma,
so negative it seemed to me.

Days turned into weeks and weeks into months.
I looked out each day, and cried, and cried.
And that was because of the look of the place,
and wondered why these gods, they cursed.

And one day, one day, one wonderful day,
as I looked out, I could not believe my eyes!
I saw buds, and sprouts, and miniature leaves.
And cried out, "My God, you restored them back!"

I Live Where Billboards Are Broken

KERRY ADAMAH KENNEDY

I live where billboards are broken
my sweet home,
where cotton blooms and snapper fish lives.
This home, where our coconut trees
know our history.
I live with mice running up and down my home.
I live here where we dance to the sound of the *Samba*,
where kola nuts and pepper welcome us.
This land, of beautiful lakes and mountains.

I live here,
where we don't hear birds chirping in the morning.
My home isn't like that.
We don't wake to the singing of birds,
but we wake to the tussle of mice in our rooms,
running, investigating,
and ripping apart our documents.

In my room, I hear two mice discuss
how they will eat my shoes.
One says he's making his lair in them.
Another says my passport on the table
is good food
so, he helps himself.

He chews on, but discovers the shoes too hard
for his old teeth. So, he stops,
and I laugh, hearing them talk,
but I'm scared to approach them.
I wake to mice running,
and my mom, making breadfruit soup
in the hot morning.

Home

KERRY ADAMAH KENNEDY

I hear the coconut trees moving against the wind
against my face,
of the potholes, the coal-tar down the avenue
of the sea, its silence that speaks of the weather,
its calmness in the wind.

Of the earth, they speak, telling of the blood
they've seen shed here on this shore, this Monrovia.
Of how men were killed, women, raped,
and babies, ripped from
their mothers' wombs.
Liberia, home, the Atlantic. Home.

Of the buildings, they speak, telling how
buildings bore bullets to their sides,
of how it was home to child soldiers,
and how mothers were beaten, boys like me,
sodomized,
and turned into drug addicts.

Of the soil, they speak, telling stories of its richness,
of how crops would grow after the war.
And they speak of how we still thrive here
on cassavas, potatoes, watermelons,
pineapples, coconuts.
I hear the coconut trees speak to the wind,
this land, this still sweet land of liberty.

Water Birds

JANETTA KONAH

The water birds come from afar
just at the break of dawn
when the patchy sky is gray-blue
and the sun is not yet fully aglow
nor have the clouds rolled out
their icy white carpets up yonder.

They come and settle
in the grassy green fields
where the dew sinks low
in wet little droplets.

The mist is dim, but those water birds
five or six, sometimes even ten
flutter their slender wings or stand idle
with outstretched necks and long legs.
They stroll leisurely in the low grass,
by the river, their white feathers glisten
against the dullness of daybreak.

They move to make no sound
in the peace and newness of the day.
It is a fascinating sight to see.
Even little children gather
singing, "Water birds, water birds,
please give us white fingers."

Repeatedly, they dance and chant
watching the birds flap their wings.
Enjoying the attention, the birds whoosh
slightly into the air and swoosh back down,
performing some mystic aerobics.

And when the morning light seeps
through the blue of the skyline,
they take off, leaving the children
with white spots on their fingernails.

My Grieving Mother

JANETTA KONAH

My mother wails in the wind
above the raging sea.

On a cold, cold dark night,
she turns in on herself
like the waves of the sea tearing up itself.
One crash after the other,
one blow follows another.

Till fissures grow on her strong walls,
and torrents of emotions build,
and rise up inside her,
stirring a storm of sorrows.

A memory long gone, comes back
to haunt her as if it were the Mano river
emptying itself into the Atlantic ocean.

My mother in a dimly lit room,
folds herself, and mourns
biting back the abandonment.

A woman, forgotten by the man
she has given her everything,
and now, she's become a barren field,
pulsing with silence.

I know, she still hears the retreating
steps of my father.
The banging of the door
that brings in gusts of cold wind,
and that long lost memory which plays
on a loop in her mind.
She tries so I do not see
the prickling pains numbing her heart.
But her scream is the howling wind
above the sea in the dead of night.

Memorabilia

JANETTA KONAH

In the left corner
of our big family piazza,
the rocking chair sits alone
devoid of the body
that once pressed against it.

I wonder if it misses the warmth of Mama,
how she sat there from dawn to dusk
softly rocking back and forth
with my baby sister Tomah in her arms.

It has been five years
and no one has sat there
to rock its limbs, sing soft songs in Kru
to a baby snuggled in their chest.

This old raggedy chair
that helped Mama rock
each one of us when we were babies
must know Tomah is grown.

It must be cold,
must scream in silent agony,
must understand the pain
of letting go when you still yearn to hold on.

I wonder if like every mother,
this chair doesn't want to let us grow up

doesn't wish to let us retire
from its semi-form of motherhood.

It sits so still but sturdy
like it is holding onto a distant hope,
a wish for a newborn baby
carved in its corners,
but Tomah was the last of us.

The Life of a Poet

NVASEKIE KONNEH

For Bai T. Moore

He carries society's heavy load
on this rocky and bumpy road.
But those for whom he toils
know not that he lives in neglect.
What's the essence of fighting
to free and enlighten an entrapped people
who don't care about your feelings,
and will only cause you more grief?
What an unkind and ungrateful treatment
for such a worthy self-denial and sacrifice
by a poet who is ever persistent
in the cause of peace and justice?
How could a life be worth living
in an environment that's so degenerating.

My Father's Last Prayer

NVASEKIE KONNEH

He was the kind of father
whose love for his children was deeper
than all the oceans combined
though he did not weave that love
into a suit that we could wear proudly.
We have loving mothers (his four wives)
whose motherly love nurtured us
to be the strong men and women
we have grown to be.
Since we could not fashion his love
into a crown that we could wear with pride,
we doubted if he ever loved us.
As he approached his final hours
I discovered this hidden love
I could not see all these years.
He wrapped this love with sincere prayer
placed it in my hands, and told me
to share with my brothers and sisters.
While I felt elevated to the seventh sky
that he had finally crowned me,
I felt guilty for holding back the love
that I should have embraced him with.
All because of the feeling of being under-loved
when he was well and alive.
While I dutifully cared for him on his dying bed,
the feeling of not being loved
stood as an invisible wall between us
till he demolished it with his last words of prayer.

Rock Your Jaws

LEKPELE M. NYAMALON

Food was scarce
like gemstones, hard to come by.
Everyone looked drained
skinned to the last sight of ribs,
feeble men, like miners, held shovels
shoveling the depths of the earth
searching for the prized Palm Kernels.

Rock your jaws,
rock your jaws,
rock your jaws
with palm kernels,
the vendor's voice echoed.

Everyone rushed to buy.
Soon, everyone was rocking
taste and money didn't matter.
The strongest lived.

Rock your jaws and live
chew the pulp,
and hang onto life.
Rock your jaws . . .
The vendor sold life.

You Post Stockade

LEKPELE M. NYAMALON

Don't smile at me.
I was kept in your basement
like a rabbit,
but you never budged.

Fed like a rat
while you only looked on.
Beaten with cartridges,
but you only looked away.

Why now?
Do you need a friend?
Keep doing your thing.
No one cares.

I dread your name
You know it
You can't grip me
Not anymore

Say Nothing

When you reach the tree, say nothing
For what do the dead know of living?
With gouged insides and aching smiles,
stay mute

Hush, be silent
Let the tide ebb sorrow
as the cotton tree shades death
Say nothing

Let death tiptoe by
with anger in its wake
See them hurl questions.
The dead knows nothing

of laughter and of life
Love too painful to remember
lies too real to forget.
Why ask the dead

who walks the earth
searching for life?
Let your eyes speak
of remembered days

And aching nights
Say nothing
For what do the dead know?
Hush.

Sing to Me, Ade

On Reading "Praise Song for My Children"

EUNICE SUA SEYAKER

For Ade (Patricia Jabbeh Wesley)

Sing to me, Ade.
I listen with yearning ears,
sing to me.

Up the Ducor hill,
I stand in awe
of the pepper birds, silenced
at the crack of a new dawn.

The ocean rises, and falls
and Ducor Hill descends to the lowland
and the mangrove swamp
to quietly bury my stories in arts
and the mud of the past.

So, sing the Tales
of liberation fighters—Like JJ Roberts
whose threats with bullets
and a cannon
gave birth to this dream.

No, the dirge, Ade!
Help me mourn my father
whose blood was fed to this soil
to keep injustice aglow.

I have searched for my father's glory
on Google, and in libraries,

but all I find are fragmented, molded stories,
raked of truth, soaked in lies.

I am the true meaning of loss,
a seed that sprang on foreign soil.
Help me trace my roots
from where it enters my background.

Sing to me, Ade, yes, we
are the children you sing.

Ashes of My Heart

LAMELLE SHAW

Although my body should lie
covered here in chipping stone
my grave holds not my soul
nor my decaying bones.
Sure, it has a tombstone
saying "Rest in Peace,"
but the grave has no corpse
lying at its feet.

My soul has been charred;
my flesh, cremated
ashes, shared among those
I loved and hated.
I've left them all
for somewhere better,
but to you, my darling,
I left a love letter,
proclaiming my love
till death do us part
in an envelope containing
the ashes of my heart.

Nomad Child

MOHAMED SHERIFF

My ancestors move in my mind
like a herd of cattle
from Egypt to Sierra Leone
through the beaten path
of my father's words
upon my ears—

Tales of people speaking a serpent's tongue
that talk to god and turn men into beasts

Beside his words is my mother always affixed
who too, came from travelers—
crossed great waters
separating Barbados from Liberia

They together birthed land seekers
housed in America's belly
looking back

The First Heartbeat

MOHAMED SHERIFF

We were told to hit our heels
against the deck

without ever hearing its sound—
nor ever feeling the fluid of the ground

teaching us to march

We couldn't fully fashion the boots
around our toes or their coming days together

We only moved against
a thud then

to the tune of generations before us—
ground whisperers that seduced concrete

with a unison that mocked melody

The island's sun beating on us
teaching a language also spoken in our chests

"Left right, low right," he commanded

And once we learned to sing with our legs
we stayed in-step and went to war

That rhythm not unlike the Marine's Anthem

Tragedies

JOSHUA T. G. SMITH

All over all around, all I see
are tragedies
From hungry families to kids sleeping
on the streets
Little by little, my fear rises while
my hope decreases
Another girl is raped, but the rapist
is released
Diabolism has reached its peak, so
I'm not at ease
Johnny got missing days ago, and today
he's found dead by the sea
The world is good, the world is bad
What should I believe?
The wicked sits at the top, and the righteous
are found beneath
The words I hear my pastor preach don't
give me hope again
A time of comfort will come
for those that mourn
Until then, all over the world,
all I see are tragedies

Let's Be Cool

PRINCE U. D. TARDEH

I know you've been the one putting fire on my roof
and wasting water in my soup.
I'm grateful for how you decided
to tear apart my couch
and sink my bed with your loops.

Thanks to those days you shoved me against
the rocks in my yard
that bruised my bald.
You were the one who pulled me naked
and dug out my old clothes from the grave.
I admire the way your lips winked like pepper birds,
singing songs of stories for my sorrow.

You dusted my eyes
and gave me rain that washed me.
My heart is a crystal you can now see.

Hope you can see the color of my rainbow
as it sets over the ocean floor,
as the sun gives light to my moon.

Hope you can come and take a share
of my light under my torn roof.
Let's bury your black face, and set up for a date.
Let's kick the doors of hatred, and eat from love's plate.
Wishing we would dine together
and toss our glasses of wine.
Let's hold our hands,
dance, and cover our faces at pretense.

Red Light

AUGUSTINE F. TAYLOR JR.

At Relight Market, there are lots of things,
to smile, laugh and get angry about.
Businesspeople occupy the streets of Relight
and pedestrians can't move freely.
Vehicles sitting in traffic,
the order of the day.

Dirty streets of Relight.
During the rainy season
mud overtakes the streets.
Wearing your boots, you can
be swallowed by mud.

Relight is dangerous at night.
Criminals roam the streets, and people
are often hijacked, their phones and money
stolen by those criminals.
Most people are frightened by Relight.
Relight is like death.

Earth's a Battlefield

AYOUBA TOURE

when life gives ten reasons
why you should walk off the earth,
give a hundred reasons to stay.
it's not every tree that gets uprooted
in the storm.
you're not dust that should dance
to the beat of any wind.
and there will be more storms.
plant your feet in a way
that after the tsunami, you'll remain
unmoved. grandma says, we crawl
into the world with clenched fists
because earth is a boxing ring.
we must busy ourselves, dodging punches
life throws at us.

On Searching for Peace from Within

AYOUBA TOURE

dear flower / it's been a while since i last watered you / since i last washed dust off your branches / too long since i halt plucking out weeds that are hindering your growth / & for so long i have let passersby trample you. / i know that you have been learning how to die / under a cold and isolated roof / that i left you. i swear / i have lost count of the last time i tended to you. / truth is, i have been occupied with absolutely nothing / truth is, i have been choking myself to death for no reasons / truth is, i have been fooling myself that i am not a good gardener / to look after you / & to protect your soft parts from being hurt by the sharp ones / truth is, all these years, i have been searching for a pearl / that is only found in you / & i blame myself for escorting you to the edge of this cliff / i damn myself for looking for something that i will only find / in the flower inside the heart of my mirror / i still don't get it that i abandoned you only / to seek a hand from strangers / when i know that even my shadow will someday break up with me / unlock its fingers from mine / & leave me in the dark / when i know that you're the only one who can love me / more than any once-barren lady would love her first child. / & this is me drowning / in regrets / this is me coming back to kiss / & swallow all your thorns / this is me lighting up the firewood / so all the cold / & stiffness in your house will be burnt / to nothingness / this is me saying that you're enough / enough to stretch my mouth into a perpetual smile / this is me saying you will blossom / into three times the acres of amazon / this is me saying you will come up just fine / like a new dawn, after every stumble / this is me saying you will rise / & your branches will make undying love / to the sky / this is me saying you will soar / like an eagle, no matter the pressure of the wind / & this is me saying whenever i am lost, i will begin to find myself in myself / & not the guy behind the other door.

The Women of Monrovia Are Citizens of Heaven

AYOUBA TOURE

Lost in His thoughts, perplexed
on what to make the blueprint
of the next gender;
God turned to the shore of Monrovia,
gathered in his hands some dust
and blew life into it.

I used to curse Adam
for stupidly falling prey to a lady's words
until I met a girl from this shore;
where God got the recipe for Eve's body.

Only a smile from her
I jumped and touched God's throne;
Only a touch from her
&
all the storms in my house cease to exist.

Rebirth

AYOUBA TOURE

there you are contemplating
on beautifying your wrist with a semicolon;
yearning to be baptized into a river of jordan,
that mustn't bring you back on shore
once it has swallowed you; your legs are itching
to kick the stool still keeping your name in mouths.
by god, i do not wear the skin that covers your bones,
neither do i know the taste of all the scars
that have made home on them &
i do not know how to get the weak or the dead
back on two legs, but i do know
we're gold walking through a tunnel: *fire*
that leads us all to beautiful transitions.

The Home in Ruin

KULAH K. WASHINGTON

The smell of baked butter cookies,
and the taste of the sweetest potato greens
I have ever tasted, greets me as I walk
past the heart of our home—the kitchen.

Now stands as a house in ruin,
the bricks falling as leaves in the dry season.
The roof that was once the prettiest of them
all has vanished into thin air.

My room shows me the spots where my portraits
as a child, hung, but all I see now
is the hollowing sea that lies beyond.

It was a beautiful place; the warmth brought families,
families brought children, and children brought friends
and girlfriends, but how can a girlfriend come
without her family and her family,
without their family?
What was once a beautiful place
is now a house in ruin.

Peace

VERMON WASHINGTON

Sunset
Chills from the whirling harmattan breeze.
   Calm hovers
        over Liberia
as I look up at Mount Nimba,
   all I think about is peace
from stray bullets to manned missiles,
   from Sudan to Yemen and all—
All I think about is peace, be still . . .

If We Could Love Again

VERMON WASHINGTON

If we could love again,
the earth would pause her rotations,
daylight and darkness will hug,
galaxies of kindness will rise.

If we could love again,
joy will overflow our hearts,
race will not be a word in the dictionary,
as we move past our past.

If we could love again,
we will embrace the future,
the world will be a happy place.
If we could love again.

Monrovia Vagrants

OTHELLO WEH

Nobody knows their names.
They go from club to club, block to block,
walking about aimless, like a car
without brakes, until daybreak.
When they hear "Police!"
they run like frightened dogs.

They live a zigzag lifestyle,
get high as the sky.
Everybody talks about them.
Nobody cares about them.
Very pretty, helpless and sleepless,
they drink gin or whisky
hustle to make ends meet,
and make Monrovia a bustling city.

You find their bodies in strange places,
but no attorneys pick up their homicide cases.

Oh, the notorious *zogoes*.
From the slums,
they stand at street corners.
They stand in the dark
hiding like predators,

ready to pounce on their prey.
With knives in their pockets,
with scissors in their jackets,
ready to rob or rape.

Everybody talks about them.
You find their bodies in strange places.
But no attorneys pick up their homicide cases.

Sit Down

OTHELLO WEH

Boys and girls, sit down,
sit down.
When your pa says, "Sit down,"
sit down.
When your ma says, "Sit down,"
sit down.

If you don't sit down
unwanted pregnancy
will make you sit down,
or your strict grandpa
will make you sit down
or the midnight police
will make you sit down.

Sit down
when your ma says,
"Sit down!"

Monrovia Flood

OTHELLO WEH

Thank you yah flood water.
Thank you for cleaning our streets.
Look at the plastic bags, the empty cups,
the bananas and orange peelings in your river.

You rush downtown
wash, clean up the town
in anger.

You work without pay.
Only God will pay you.

Never mind yah, never mind.
The feces are washed away,
and so are the plastic bottles, soiled diapers,
cucumber, and plantain peelings.

Flood water, oh, you work tirelessly
to sweep downtown, to clean up the town.
In rage and annoyance,
you work without pay.
Only God will pay you.

Sorry for our attitudes oooooo.
Look at us, young and old,

rich and poor, men and women,
we remove dirt from our cars, our homes
and dump them in the streets.

We throw everything anywhere.
We keep the streets dirty
and public places filthy.

Oh, flood water, you work without pay.
Only God will pay you.

The Secrets of September

KORTO WILLIAMS

*The light easily flowed through her crumpled blue gown that ended at
her feet*
with a mask of pride, tight over her face.
*She smiled at no one, and remembered that she got that dress during the
OAU conference, 1979.*
She was ready to tell her story.

Long ago, she says in a hoarse and hollow voice,
our people died in faraway countries and in a shipyard.
This is a story of unbroken love, death, and joining with the ancestors.
This was a time when people
asked each other in whispers
How do we go on when we do not know if we are alive?
The hum in the room got louder.
and she sat in the center, worried about the eyes on her back.
She starts again.

He told me he was dead.
Safe from the secrets of September.
She said, "Stay with me until this torture ends."
September was the time
when the earth gobbled our people like a hungry man with lots of
shillings,
eating *nyamachoma*, chased by hot Tusker on that slipway near
Waiyaki Way.
The memory remains etched in our hearts, and on huts in our villages
and cities.
The curl at the top of our lips missing when we pretended to smile

cheeks spreading, but the light from our eyes shut by a dull veil of fear.
We knew we could not betray the secrets of September.
They were powerful and violent.
And we dare not speak of August,
when the thrust into the black soil was forced.

September came
and swallowed the unprepared.
Our tears sat in puddles on gaunt cheeks,
forcibly willing a reversal of this pain.
Saltiness that stings
formed trails from the table made by a tired carpenter
to the floor with layers of dirt, sounds of guns, and *tah-bayed* people
    screams.

There was murmuring in the room.
The rain hit the windows.
And rushed like tears to come.
The woman crouched in fear, and pain.
She spoke in a staccato fashion.
With shots, they bowed and fell.
Loyal souls were stolen.
Like rotted tree boughs, they fell
with no last words
to the ones whose prayers
were a chorus of their names
as they wailed in Babylon.

A sigh comes from deep in the hearts of the people.
She slips from the chair,
and is in a fetal position, telling the story.

The others found refuge in a place of healing
believing in Phebe to take that letter of Paul,

seeking salvation.
Ahh September!
They were killed and rotted
with only hair and skeleton on each hospital bed and in hallways.
They were dumped into the brown earth
to the muddy discomfort of a mass grave
wet and laced with lightning shine.

This part was hard
tears flowed, and no one knew who owned them.
She looked up, into their faces,
and told of her brother and how he escaped to die in Mandela's land.
She continued.

In faraway places
September fought.
They screamed—That is not how we say goodbye.
Someone said he could not love you and die before you.
He slowly slid away
but he held onto the world with all his strength.
Holding on to familiarity—his ring and Bible,
laughter, the smile of surrender and sadness,
memories of life phases.
Oh! That time when they walked under the moonlight to Gbenyahn
    Town.
He held on to the light he saw when he held his first child.
On a bed, white around him,
faces, linen, light
September won.

She stops crying, resigned to the reality.

The people got a wooden box and a body.
His spirit remained and learned Azania's songs and dances.

He watched people float and hit the ground, bringing vibrations.
He learned to lift his voice in a dirge for self.
He danced as Mama Miriam sang,
the lion sleeps tonight. In a strange land.
Nomzamo poured a libation of gin
and led him to his women ancestors.
They had come to meet his spirit.
White cotton hair, wet with saltwater
mud on their gowns, they had escaped holes to meet him,
cleaning the sand under their fingernails
eyes blazing with bliss
pudgy arms reached out.
She joined them as they enveloped his tired body.
She quietly said,
There isn't any pain I haven't known.
In his voice.

She becomes still.
The people draw their chairs closer to the center.
She is afraid of the eyes on her back.
She ends the story.

I have said the secrets in daylight.
We do not speak of the ones who left in August.
Our silence nurtures the grief and broken heart.
To the ones who took their last breath near the ships,
and the ones who were dumped in the muddy graves
dumped in the wet, dark holes,
dug by their children's hand and tears.
To the one who rests in a faraway land
we die every day to save ourselves.

As If I Never Left

MASNOH WILSON

Dried fish, pig's feet, fresh fish
damp, wet, smelly odors
stale, rancid, reeking air.
Bitter balls, *kittely*, eggplant, peppers
leafy greens, cassava leaves, collard greens
as far as the eyes can see,
freshly cut, just ground, spread all over tabletops.
I cannot believe I am standing in this place
hearing the noise all around, the sounds of cars, trucks
pen-pen, feet moving, people moving, everywhere
all around, sounds of laughter and busy feet
movements everywhere, light rain falling
with mud everywhere.
But I'm just standing still,
caught in the moment
relishing the sounds, trying not to miss a thing.
Just standing there for a moment or so
as we bantered back and forth
as I'm trying to buy from everyone
who has something to sell.
When it suddenly dawned on me,
"I've never really left this place."

And in that instant, for a minute or so
I was transported to a time,
a time that lives in infamy,
when Liberia quietly and peacefully slept
on the tranquil West African shores. . . .

SOURCE ACKNOWLEDGMENTS

EARLY LIBERIAN POETRY, 1800–1959

Hilary Teage, "Land of the Mighty Dead," previously published in *Liberia Herald* 12, no. 2. © December 23, 1842.

Hilary Teage, "Hymn," previously published in *Poems of Liberia: 1836–1961*, ed. A. Doris Banks Henries (London: Macmillan and Company, 1963).

Daniel Bashiel Warner, "All Hail, Liberia Hail," adopted in 1847 as Liberian national anthem.

Daniel Bashiel Warner, "Wishing to Be '21,'" previously published in, *Poems of Liberia 1836–1961*, ed. A. Doris Henries (London: Macmillan and Company, 1963). © Daniel Bashiel Warner.

Robert H. Gibson, "Heavenly Rest Implored," "Rise, Take Up Thy Bed and Walk," "Song of the First Emigrants to Cape Palmas," previously published in *Poems of Liberia 1836–1961*, ed. A. Doris Banks Henries (London: Macmillan and Company, 1963). © 1854 by Robert H. Gibson.

Anonymous, "St Paul's River Liberia," previously published in *Liberia Herald* 5, no. 9 (February 8, 1855): 21.

Pierre, "The Emigrant's Hymn," previously published *Liberia Herald* 7, no. 1 (July 1, 1857): 4. © 1857 by Pierre.

Edwin James Barclay, "The Lone Star: A National Song," "To Pauline—a Flirt," "To Lygia," "To Jealous Lygia," "Human Greatness," "Afric's Lament," "The Race-Soul," "The Ocean's Roar," "Dawn," "Song of the

Harmattan," "The Past," from *Leaves from Love's Garden and Random Poems* (Monrovia, Liberia: College of West Africa Press, 1910). © 1910 by Edwin James Barclay.

LIBERIAN POETRY, 1960–1989

Rev. Father James David Kwee Baker, "O Maryland! Dear Maryland!," "Land of the Beautiful," "Cavalla Grand," "Ode to Cape Mount," "Divine Guidance," previously published in *Poems of Liberia 1836–1961*, ed. A. Doris Banks Henries (London: Macmillan and Company, 1963). © 1963 by Rev. Father James David Kwee Baker. Used by permission of Yede Baker Dennis (for the Rev. Father James David Kwee Baker Estate, May 2021).

Roland Tombekai Dempster, "Is This Africa," "Africa's Plea," "The Lone Star Shines," "When You Die—a Philosophy of Life," "The Poet's Ear," "Take the World Away, but Give Me Freedom," "Go On and Do, Let the People Talk," "To Man," "The Pepper Bird Is Singing," "Liberia in Verse and Song," previously published in *Echoes from the Walley: Being Odes and Other Poems*, ed. Roland Tombekai Dempster, Bai T. Moore, and H. Carey Thomas (Monrovia, Liberia: D. Muir Print. Office, 1947). © 1947 by Roland T. Dempster. And from *A Song Out of Midnight by Roland* (Morovia, Liberia: Independently published by T. Dempster). © Roland T. Dempster.

H. Carey Thomas, "A Sonnet—the Poet's Soul," "Ask Me Why," "No Longer Yesterday," "Because You Told Me," "When You Sigh," "At Sunset," "Echoes of a Longing Heart," "The Tom-Toms Beat No More," from *Echoes from the Valley: Being Odes and Other Poems*, ed. Roland Tombekai Dempster, Bai T. Moore, and H. Carey Thomas Dempster (Monrovia, Liberia: D. Muir Print. Office, 1947). © 1947 by H. Carey Thomas. Used by permission, Harmon Carey Thomas (for H. Carey Thomas Estate).

Bai T. Moore, "Ebony Dust," "Monrovia Market Women," "Africa in Retrospect," "The Legend of Shad Tubman," "A Wingless Bird," "My Africa," "The Bulldozer," "The Hallelujah Stuff," "Yana Boys," "The Strength of a Nation," "Ko Bomi hee m koa," "Ba nya m go koma," from *Ebony Dust*,

2nd ed. (Monrovia, Liberia: Ducor Publishing House, 1976). © 1962 by Bai T. Moore. Used by permission of Sando Moore (for the Bai T. Moore Estate, September 25, 2020).

Kona Khasu (James Roberts), "Dear Patrice Lumumba," "Our Man on Broad Street," "Unnamed Thing," "Their Words—Deception," "To Time Our Enemy," "The Old Stream," from *The Seeds of Time: A Collection of Poems*, University of Zurich, "English Department: The Liberian Literature Project," https://www.es.uzh.ch/en/Subsites/Projects/liberianliteratureproject/konakhasu.html. © 1971 by Kona Khasu (James Roberts). Used by permission of Kona Khasu (James Roberts, 2021).

CONTEMPORARY LIBERIAN POETRY, 1900–PRESENT

Althea Romeo-Mark, "Who's on Watch?," "Visiting Khufu," "Oya (Wind in Cape Town)," "A Different Kind of Pied Piper 2020," "The Cat-Gods Have Fallen." Used by permission of author.

Patricia Jabbeh Wesley, "Praise Song for My Children," "November 12, 2015," "What Took Us to War," "When Monrovia Rises," "I Want to Be the Woman," "Biography When the Wanderers Come Home," "We Departed Our Homelands and We Came," "An Elegy for the St. Peter's Church Massacre," "They Want to Rise Up," "Monrovia Women," from *Praise Song for My Children: New and Selected Poems* (Pittsburgh: Autumn House Press, 2020). © 2020 by Patricia Jabbeh Wesley. Used by permission, Autumn House Press.

Patricia Jabbeh Wesley, "Pittsburgh," "I'm Waiting," previously published in *Vox Populi* magazine, December 9, 2020, and March 24, 2021. © 2021 by Patricia Jabbeh Wesley. Used by permission of *Vox Populi*.

EMERGING AND ASPIRING LIBERIAN POETS

Barth Akpah, "Harper Nedee?," "Oche Dike Ala (Grandma Has Gone)." Used by permission of author.

Jee-Won Mawein Esika Arkoi, "A Woman," "If." Used by permission of author.

Jee-Won Mawein Esika Arkoi, "My Mother's Tale," previously published in *One World, One People: 2019 DoveTales Anthology*, ed. Patricia Jabbeh

Wesley (Fort Collins CO: Writing for Peace, 2019). © by Jee-Won Marwein Esika Arkoi. Used by Permission.

Watchen Johnson Babalola, "While Tomorrow Waits," "Divided We Stand." Used by permission of author.

Edwin Olu Bestman, "New Kru Town, Where I Come From," "Darkness, the Surname of a Poor Lover," previously published in *Spillwords*, September 16, 2020. © Edwin Olu Bestman. Used by permission of author.

Edwin Olu Bestman, "How to Write a Dirge for Liberia," previously published in *Spillwords*, October 20, 2020. © Edwin Olu Bestman. Used by permission of author.

Edward K. Boateng, "Memories of Home," "Genealogy of the Fourteen Pieces of Liberia," previously published in *Ngagi Review*, March 1, 2021. © 2021. Used by permission of author.

Edward K. Boateng, "Curing My Mother's Wound," "Maybe I'll Go Home." Used by permission of author.

Tetee Alexandra Bonar, "He Stole a Piece of Me." Used by permission of author.

Chorlyn E. Chor, "Identity." Used by permission of author.

Sunny Eddie Crawford, "You Are Mine," previously published in *Ngagi Review*, March 30, 2021. © by Sunny Eddie Crawford. Used by permission of author.

Sunny Eddie Crawford, "Words in Portrait," previously published in *Spillwords*, March 17, 2021. © by Sunny Eddie Crawford. Used by permission of author.

Arthur Shedrick Davies, "Deepu: A Definition of Divinity," previously published in *Sleepless in Monrovia* (March 2021). © 2021 by Arthur Shedrick Davies. Used by permission.

Arthur Shedrick Davies, "Origins of the Poet Next Door," "This Is Poetry." Used by permission of author.

Maureen Jennifer Davies, "Free Me." Used by permission of author.

Essah Cozett Diaz, "Our Mother Is Gold," "When a Rolling Stone Leaves Pebbles Behind," "For Daughters Who May Never Be Mothers," "For Women Who Are Water in Fields of Rice," "From Coal Pots to Gas Stoves," "I Wasn't Ready to Open My Eyes." Used by Permission of author.

Mawata Dukuly, "The Brown Beauty," "Who Is a Leader?" Used by permission of author.

James Varney Dwalu, "The Oppressed," "I Am Nothing (Neutrality)." Used by permission of author.

Cynthia Senu Gailor, "Where Were You?" Used by permission of author.

Daniel W. Garteh Jr., "Quarantine in Hope." Used by permission of author.

Cherbo Geeplay, "Africa," previously published in *Adelaide* 3 (July 2018). © 2018 by Cherbo Geeplay. Used by permission of author.

Aloysius S. Harmon, "The Diary of an Orphan," "Pain as Metaphor," "West Point, Liberia." Used by permission of author.

Ruby M. Harmon, "Nah Fooh, Nah Fooh," "Grey Stone Blues," "Mother and Daughter." Used by permission of author.

Quita Harvey, "We Need to Pass It On." Used by permission of author.

Laurel Iloani, "One World, One People," previously published in *One World, One People: 2019 DoveTales Anthology*, ed. Patricia Jabbeh Wesley (Fort Collins CO: Writing for Peace, 2019). © 2019 by Laurel Iloani. Used by permission of author.

Patrice Juah, "The Ebola Ride," from *Under Ducor Skies* (Lawrencefille GA: Village Tales Publishing). © 2018 by Patrice Juah.

Patrice Juah, "An Afro-Madrileña Love Note," previously published by IE Foundation Prizes in Humanities, Madrid, Spain. Used by permission of author.

McChen A. D. Kanneo, "Ebony Perfection." Used by permission of author.

Jeremy Teddy Karn, "The Making of Grief," "Elegy for a Friend." Used by permission of author.

Evelyn Kehleay-Miller, "My First Winter." Used by permission of author.

Kerry Adamah Kennedy, "I Live Where Billboards Are Broken," previously published in *One World, One People: 2019 DoveTales Anthology*, ed. Patricia Jabbeh Wesley (Fort Collins CO: Writing for Peace, 2019).

Kerry Adamah Kennedy, "Home." Used by permission of author.

Janetta Konah, "Water Birds," "My Grieving Mother." Used by permission of author.

Janetta Konah, "Memorabilia," previously published in *Eboquill Literary*, March, 6, 2021. Used by permission.

Nvasekie Konneh, "The Life of a Poet," "My Father's Last Prayer." Used by permission of author.

Lekpele M. Nyamalon, "Rock Your Jaws," "You Post Stockade." Used by permission of author.

Jackie Sayegh, "Say Nothing." Used by permission of author.

Eunice Sua Seyaker, "Sing to Me, Ade: On Reading 'Praise Song for My Children.'" Used by permission of author.

Lamelle Shaw, "Ashes of My Heart." Used by permission of author.

Mohamed Sheriff, "Nomad Child," "The First Heartbeat." Used by permission of author.

Joshua T. G. Smith, "Tragedies." Used by permission of author.

Prince U. D. Tardeh, "Let's Be Cool." Used by permission of author.

Augustine F. Taylor Jr., "Red Light." Used by permission of author.

Ayouba Toure, "Earth's a Battlefield," "On Searching for Peace from Within," "The Women of Monrovia Are Citizens of Heaven," "Rebirth." Used by permission of author.

Kulah K. Washington, "The Home in Ruin," from *One World, One People: 2019 DoveTales Anthology*, ed. Patricia Jabbeh Wesley (Fort Collins CO: Writing for Peace, 2019). Used by permission of author.

Vermon Washington, "Peace," "If We Could Love Again." Used by permission of author.

Othello Weh, "Monrovia Vagrants," "Sit Down," "Monrovia Flood." Used by permission of author.

Korto Williams, "The Secrets of September," from *Inappropriate Medley: Intersections Between Patriarchy, Pleasure and Redemption* (Johannesburg, South Africa: Ssali, 2020). © 2020 by Korto Williams. Used by permission of author.

Masnoh Wilson, "As If I Never Left." Used by permission of author.

CONTRIBUTORS

Hilary Teage (1802–May 21, 1853) was a Liberian merchant, journalist, and politician in the early years of the republic. Born in the state of Virginia in the United States, he was prominent in early Liberian colonial politics. He advocated for Liberia's independence from the American Colonization Society. He is credited for drafting the Declaration of Independence. Like most of the Liberia's early politicians, he also wrote poetry in his spare time.

Daniel Bashiel Warner (April 19, 1815–December 1, 1880) was the third president of Liberia from 1864 to 1868. Prior to that, he also served as vice president and secretary of state. He was the author of the lyrics for the Liberian national anthem.

Robert H. Gibson (1838–?), according to scanty biographical details from Maryland State Archives, left Baltimore with his family on the schooner *Harmony* on June 28, 1835, and arrived at Cape Palmas, Liberia, on August 23, 1835. Robert, sometimes known as Henry, lost his father the following year and his mother remarried. Henry was still living with his mother and likely lived with her until her death in 1847.

Anonymous—unknown poet whose poems appeared in the *Liberia Herald* in the 1850s.

Pierre was a Liberian poet who signed his poems under the name Pierre and published poetry in the *Liberia Herald* in 1850s.

Edwin James Barclay (January 5, 1882–November 6, 1955) was a politician, poet, and musician who served as the eighteenth president of Liberia. The most important poet of the times, Barclay explored every aspect of the early Liberian life, including his love life, the political climate, and the struggles of the nation. His most famous was the "Lone Star," the national patriotic song still sung today.

LIBERIAN POETRY, 1960–1989

Rev. Father James David Kwee Baker was one of the nation's most outstanding clergymen and founder of St. Thomas Episcopal Church on Camp Johnson Road, Monrovia. He was born to Grebo parents at Hoffman Station, Maryland County, on June 17, 1893. He received his early education at St. Augustine's Boarding School at Cuttington Collegiate Divinity School (the primary division of Cuttington College and Divinity School), after which Cuttington College was established in 1889 by the Protestant Episcopal Church during the episcopacy of the church's great education bishop Rt. Rev. Samuel David Ferguson.

Roland Tombekai Dempster (1910–1965) was one of the most prolific Liberian poets since Edwin James Barclay, authoring a diversity of poems, which, though after the Western literary tradition, celebrated the Liberia of Dempster's time. He was born in Tosoh (on the banks of Lake Piso), Grand Cape Mount County, Liberia. He is the author of *The Mystic Reformation of Gondolia* (1953), and in 1960 he published *A Song Out of Midnight: Souvenir of the Tubman-Tolbert Inauguration* celebrating President William V. S. Tubman.

H. Carey Thomas (Harmon Carey Thomas, 1910–1980) was born in Brewerville, Montserrado County, Liberia. He studied at the then Liberia College and was a poet, lawyer, and member of Liberia's House of Representatives. He also served in many capacities in the Liberian government while composing poetry. H. Carey, as he was affectionately called, was one of the many victims of Liberia's first military coup in 1980, arrested on April 12, 1980, and imprisoned with other government officials. On April 30, 1980, he was killed while in custody of the new military government and buried with dozens of other Liberian officials in a mass grave.

Bai T. Moore (Bai Tamia Johnson Moore, October 12, 1916–January 10, 1988) was a Liberian poet, novelist, folklorist, and essayist. He held various governmental positions in the Liberian government and for UNESCO. One of the strongest advocates of Liberian culture, Moore founded Liberia's National Cultural Center during his tenure as deputy minister of tourism in the Information Ministry. His books include a novella, *Murder in the Cassava Patch* (1968), a book of poems, *Ebony Dust* (1962), and *The Money Doubler* (1976). He, Roland T. Dempster, and H. Carey Thomas collaborated and co-authored a Liberian poetry collection, *Echoes from the Valley: Being Odes and Other Poems* (1947).

Kona Khasu (James Roberts) was born James Emmanuel Roberts in Suehn, Bomi County, in 1942 and raised in Bassa Community, Soniwehn, Jallah Town sections of Monrovia. He is a graduate of Monrovia College and holds degrees from Hobart College, Boston University, and Harvard. In the 1970s he directed the Liberian Cultural Troup at Kendejah, near Monrovia, and taught English courses at the University of Liberia for many years until the Liberian civil war. He produced and directed Liberia's first T.V series, *Kotati*, which was workshopped through Blamadon Theater. He most recently served as deputy minister of education for planning at the Ministry of Education from 2006 to 2012.

CONTEMPORARY LIBERIAN POETRY, 1990–PRESENT

Althea Romeo-Mark, born in West Indies, is an educator who grew up in St. Thomas, U.S. Virgin Island; has lived in the United States, Liberia, and the United Kingdom; and has resided in Switzerland since 1991. A founding member of the Liberian Association of Writers, she is the author of two full-length poetry collections, *The Nakedness of New* and *If Only the Dust Would Settle*; three chapbooks, *Beyond Dreams: The Ritual Dancer*, *Two Faces, Two Phases*, and *Palaver*; and a poetry collaboration, *Shu-Shu Moko Jumbi: The Silent Dancing Spirit*.

Patricia Jabbeh Wesley immigrated with her family to the United States after surviving two years of the fourteen-year series of Liberian civil wars. Her six critically acclaimed books of poetry include *Praise Song for My Children: New and Selected Poems* (2020), *When the Wanderers Come Home* (2016), *Where the Road Turns* (2010), *The River Is Rising* (2007), *Becoming Ebony* (2003), and *Before the*

Palm Could Bloom: Poems of Africa (1998). She is also the author of one children's book, *In Monrovia, the River Visits the Sea* (2012). Her poems, short stories, and memoir articles have been featured in many anthologies and magazines, including *Prairie Schooner, Transition,* the *New York Times Magazine, Harvard Review, Harvard Divinity Review,* and *Crab Orchard Review,* among others, and her work has been translated into several languages. She has won many awards, including the 2023 Theodore Roethke Memorial Poetry Prize for her sixth book of poetry, *Praise Song for My Children; Poetry Magazine's* 2022 Levinson Prize for her poems "Black Woman Selling Her Home in America" and "Healing Will Come: Elegy After Natural Disaster"; *Prairie Schooner's* Edward Stanley Prize for her poem "My Name Is Dawanyeno"; and a 2002 Crab Orchard Award for her second book, *Becoming Ebony.* Founder of Young Scholars of Liberia, an organization devoted to mentoring Liberian youth in writing and excellence, she is a professor of English, creative writing, and African literature at Penn State Altoona.

EMERGING AND ASPIRING LIBERIAN POETS

Barth Akpah (Bartholomew C. Akpah) is a literary critic, poet, and teacher. He is the author of a collection of poems, *Land of Tales.* His articles have been published in journals within and outside Africa. He currently teaches English and literature courses at William V. S Tubman University, Harper, Liberia.

Jee-Won Mawein Esika Arkoi is a student studying social work at the Stella Maris University, Mother Patern College of Health Sciences, in Monrovia, Liberia. She has been a mentee of Dr. Patricia Jabbeh Wesley with the Young Scholars of Liberia since 2018. She has published one poem, "My Mother's Tale," in *Dove Tales Anthology: One Word, One People* (2019). Jee-Won hopes to continue growing as an emerging writer.

Watchen Johnson Babalola is the author of more than thirty children's stories with contributions to projects including OYSS, CESLY, CODE, Reading Liberia, and Ministry of Education.

Edwin Olu Bestman is a young Liberian poet who resides in New Kru Town, near Monrovia, Liberia. His poetry has won him recognition both locally and internationally. His poems have been published in *Odd Magazine, Spillwords, Ngiga Review*, the *Rising Phoenix*, and elsewhere.

Edward K. Boateng is an honoree of the Gujarat Sahitya Akademi Award in collaboration with Motivational Strips and holds the Order of Shakespeare Medal from Motivational Strips. His works have appeared in *Ngiga Review, Arts Lounge, Afritondo, Spillwords, Eboquills*, and elsewhere, all under the pen name Edward K. Boateng. He holds a bachelor of arts degree in philosophy from Don Bosco Institute of Philosophy, an affiliate of the University of Ibadan, Nigeria.

Tetee Alexandra Bonar is a student of the University of Liberia studying chemistry with an emphasis in industrial science. She is an aspiring poet whose work has appeared in *Ducor Review* and *Medium*. She is a mentee of Young Scholars of Liberia.

Chorlyn E. Chor is an emerging Liberian poet and a student studying biology at the Stella Maris Polytechnic University. She attended the six-week writing workshop with Young Scholars of Liberia in the summer of 2020.

Sunny Eddie Crawford writes from Liberia. His work has been published on the *Ducor Review*, We Write Liberia, and Liberian Poet Society websites. He won the Liberian Poet Society's chapbook award in 2020 for his book *Love Away from Home*.

Arthur Shedrick Davies is an emerging writer and a spoken-word artist. His poems have appeared in the *Shallow Tales Review*, the *Ducor Review, Eboquills, Poetrypower*, and elsewhere.

Maureen Jennifer Davies is a student of the African Methodist Episcopal University studying biology with an emphasis in chemistry. She is an aspiring poet.

Essah Cozett Diaz is a Liberian American poet, born and raised in Georgia. She is currently a PhD student in Caribbean literature and languages at the University of Puerto Rico, Rio Piedras campus. Her poems have been published in several print and online publications, including Jalada Africa, the Black Fork Review,

Penumbra Online, *BIM*, *805 Lit + Art*, *Peepal Tree Press*, the *Caribbean Writer*, *PREE Lit*, *Moko Magazine*, *Interviewing the Caribbean*, and *Odradek*.

Mawata Dukuly was born on January 8, 2007. A student at the Seku Ibrahim Sheriff Elementary, Junior, and Senior High School, she began writing in March of 2020 and was enrolled in the summer writing workshops of Young Scholars of Liberia.

James Varney Dwalu writes stories for children. He has published more than twenty books for children. Dwalu is a member of the Liberia Association of Writers.

Cynthia Senu Gailor, a diaspora Liberian, obtained her high school diploma from the College of West Africa and a bachelor of science degree from the University of Liberia. She lives in Georgia, United States, with her family.

Daniel W. Garteh Jr. is an aspiring poet and spoken-word artist. He has had poems published in several online poetry magazines and is also the winner of the Liberian Poet Society's International Women's Day (2020) poetry competition.

Cherbo Geeplay was born in Pleebo, Maryland, Liberia. A pan-African poet, he writes from Alberta, Canada. His work has appeared in several poetry journals including, *Liberian Sea Breeze Journal*, the *Blue Lake Review*, and the *Adelaide Literary Magazine*, for which his poem was a finalist in the 2018 Adelaide Literary Competition.

Aloysius S. Harmon is an aspiring Liberian writer and poet from southeastern Liberia, Maryland County. He is also a student at Stella Maris Polytechnic University studying biology and chemistry. He has published poetry in *Eve Poetry Magazine*, *Eboquills*, *Spillwords*, and elsewhere.

Ruby M. Harmon is a writer and pediatrician who writes poetry about her Liberian heritage and childhood. She is the author of three poetry books, *Poetic Moves while Doctoring*, *Being in Two Volumes*, and *With Love*, and a children's book, *Dromedary and Camelot*.

Quita Harvey is an emerging writer studying civil engineering at the Stella Maris Polytechnic University. She started writing in 2020 at the Young Scholars of Liberia program and has since been working to improve her writing skills.

Laurel Iloani is an aspiring writer who has attended numerous writing workshops over three years, facilitated by Dr. Patricia Jabbeh Wesley, which have improved his craft. His poetry has been published in the *2019 DoveTales Anthology*.

Patrice Juah is a poet and writer. She is the winner of IE Humanities Prize for her poem "An Afro-Madrileña Love Note," published in Madrid, Spain. Her debut book of poems, *Under Ducor Skies*, was published in 2018.

McChen A. D. Kanneo is an emerging Liberian poet. One of his poems was published on *Spillwords*.

Jeremy Teddy Karn's work has appeared in or is forthcoming in *20.35: Contemporary African Poets Volume III Anthology*, *The Whale Road*, *Ice Floe Press*, *Up the Staircase Quarterly*, *ARTmosterrific*, *Lolwe*, *Vagabond City*, *Ghost Heart Journal*, and elsewhere. His chapbook, *Miryam Magdalit*, was selected by Kwame Dawes and Chris Abani for the 2021 New Generations of African Poets Chapbook Box Series (the African Poetry Book Fund), in collaboration with Akashic Books. He is a college student and lives in Monrovia, Liberia, West Africa.

Evelyn Kehleay-Miller has a degree in accounting and masters in management from the University of Liberia and Sullivan University, Kentucky, respectfully, and lives in the United States.

Kerry Adamah Kennedy was born on October 7, 1999. He studies history and international relations at Cuttington University in Liberia and is a young emerging Liberian writer. He is one of Young Scholars of Liberia's mentees and he is a Christian.

Janetta Konah is the author of one collection of poetry, *Beautiful Pieces: A New Dawn*, published in 2019. Her works have been featured in *KWEE* magazine and *Spillwords*. She currently resides in Monrovia, Liberia.

Nvasekie Konneh is a Liberian writer, poet, magazine publisher, and community and cultural activist whose works have been widely published in newspapers in Liberia, the United States, and Europe. He is the author of two poetry collections, *Going to War for America* and *The Love of Liberty Brought Us Together*, and a memoir of the Liberian civil war, *The Land of My Father's Birth*. He won first place in the Liberian civil war poetry competition held in Providence, Rhode Island, in 2003.

Lekpele M. Nyamalon is a poetry fellow of the Open Society Initiative of West Africa and a Mandela Washington fellow with deep interests in social and political issues. His chapbook, *Yearnings of a Traveler*, explores the themes of migration, pan-Africanism, gender, identity, war, and colonialism. He witnessed the civil war as a child and captured his experiences in his book of poetry, *Scary Dreams, an Anthology of the Liberian Civil War*.

Jackie Sayegh is a Liberian educator and writer. Her writing anchors itself in belonging, identity, and memory.

Eunice Sua Seyaker is a college student studying electrical engineering at the Liberia Electricity Corporation. She is a Young Scholars of Liberia mentee and has published work with We Write Liberia.

Lamelle Shaw is a Liberian writer based in South Africa. Her work has been featured in *Tears of Fire* by the U.S. National Library of Poetry, *Breathe into Another Voice*, an anthology of jazz poetry, and several publications, including the *Oprah* magazine and *Forbes Africa*. She is the author of *Ashes of My Heart*.

Mohamed Sheriff is a Liberian American living in Washington DC. His poetry and nonfiction writing focus on race, immigration, and war from a refugee and a U.S. Marine's perspective. He often publishes articles and interviews related to his work at the National Endowment for the Arts. He is the arts administrator of Color Network at the NEA.

Joshua T. G. Smith is an aspiring Liberian poet and spoken-word artist. He lives in Monrovia, Liberia.

Prince U. D. Tardeh is an aspiring Liberian poet, creative writer, and a finalist for the Rediscover Liberia Poetry Competition. He has had poems published in *Sleepless in Monrovia*.

Augustine F. Taylor Jr. was born in March 1977 in Liberia. He is a student at the University of Liberia studying public administration.

Abuoya Toure writes from Paynesville, Liberia. He is a poet and a worshipper of music. His works have been published in *African Writer*, *Praxis Magazine*, *Ngiga Review*, *Afritondo*, *Odd Magazine*, and elsewhere.

Kulah K. Washington is a graduate of Cuttington University with a degree in biology and chemistry. She studied poetry for three years as a Young Scholars of Liberia mentee-mentor where she pruned her writing by attending workshops.

Vermon Washington has immense interests in poetry and essay. He is a student at Stella Maris Polytechnic University studying civil engineering. He loves writing about nature.

Othello Weh is author of *The Memories of a Child Soldier*, a collection of poetry published in 1995 by the Pan African Teachers Centre, Accra, Ghana. The author of several short stories, he was born in Yila, Bong County, Liberia, and teaches at the Jake Memorial Baptist College in Monrovia, Liberia.

Korto Williams is the author of a book of poetry, *Inappropriate Medley: Intersections Between Patriarchy, Pleasure, and Redemption*, and a co-founder of Liberia Feminist Forum. Her works have appeared in *Navigating Checkpoints: The Journey of the Liberia Feminist Forum*, *Al Jazeera*, *Huffington Post*, and elsewhere.

Masnoh Wilson is a teacher, writer, and author who has had one of her poems published in an online magazine, *Aadunaa*. She is also a graduate of the University of Liberia in Liberia, West Africa, and Sacred Heart University in Fairfield, Connecticut. She currently teaches fifth grade at an elementary school in South Carolina.

*Eight New-Generation African
Poets: A Chapbook Box Set*
Edited by Kwame Dawes
and Chris Abani
(Akashic Books)

*New-Generation African Poets:
A Chapbook Box Set (Tatu)*
Edited by Kwame Dawes
and Chris Abani
(Akashic Books)

*New-Generation African Poets:
A Chapbook Box Set (Nne)*
Edited by Kwame Dawes
and Chris Abani
(Akashic Books)

*New-Generation African Poets:
A Chapbook Box Set (Tano)*
Edited by Kwame Dawes
and Chris Abani
(Akashic Books)

*New-Generation African Poets:
A Chapbook Box Set (Sita)*
Edited by Kwame Dawes
and Chris Abani
(Akashic Books)

*New-Generation African Poets:
A Chapbook Box Set (Saba)*
Edited by Kwame Dawes
and Chris Abani
(Akashic Books)

*New-Generation African Poets:
A Chapbook Box Set (Nane)*
Edited by Kwame Dawes
and Chris Abani
(Akashic Books)

To order or obtain more information on these or other University of
Nebraska Press titles, visit nebraskapress.unl.edu. For more information
about the African Poetry Book Series, visit africanpoetrybf.unl.edu.

CPSIA information can be obtained
at www.ICGtesting.com
Printed in the USA
LVHW042104150223
739587LV00003B/216